MAKING A DIFFERENCE

Making a Difference

*The Pragmatic Approach
of an Interim Manager*

Harley Lovegrove

lannoo^{campus}

© Harley Lovegrove & Publishinghouse LannooCampus, 2007

DESIGN Studio Lannoo & Peer De Maeyer
FRONT COVER IMAGE Alex Lecler & Koloriet
ILLUSTRATIONS Inigo Gutirrez (figuur 2, 4, 7, 8)
COVER PHOTOGRAPH OF HARLEY Damien Lovegrove
WEB DESIGNER AND BUILDER • www.making-a-difference.be • Erwin Geens

D/2007/45/398 – ISBN 978 90 209 7370 9 – NUR 801

Publishinghouse LannooCampus
Naamsesteenweg 201
B-3001 Leuven
www.lannoocampus.com

DEDICATION

This book is dedicated to a person who had a profound influence on both my life and my career.

George Gardner was a truly unique individual, the sales director of a UK brick company, who sadly died of a heart attack, far too young. He had motivational and management gifts that went far beyond anyone else I have ever met. He had insight into others; he noticed them; he coached them. He had faith in his staff, even the ones who seemed completely hopeless. Somehow, he found ways to motivate and guide people into achieving things way beyond their own expectations. At his funeral, the church was filled with people whose lives he had touched and - in his own way - changed forever. That day, the testimonies of the few spoke for many in the congregation. It was an enlightening experience, standing in a crowd of people at the funeral of a man who you wanted in some way to thank, only to discover that everyone around you had the same feeling. Those who could not get a seat stood in the doorway and those who could not get a standing view stood silently outside the church. I sometimes think that maybe it was all too much for his family; after all, to them he was just a family man whose joy in life was reaching out to others. I never heard a single negative word about the man, except from those who were jealous of his popularity and position - and even they loved him at heart.

When I was 26, George gave me the best advice I ever received. Most importantly, he gave me vision and showed me how I could move forward in my career. He even helped to bring this about. It is safe to say that without his influence, my life would have been very different. Today I try to emulate this fine man, not as a copy but in spirit. If, in my own small way, I can do half of what he did for others in his career, I will retire happy.

THANKS

I would like to offer my personal thanks to the following people: Kurt De Ruwe, for his encouragement and personal motivation, which enabled me to write, finish and publish this book.
To the first draft reviewers: Charley Crouch, Werner Peiffer and Jean Paul Schupp.
Kristien Hansebout, who was a great help in finding a publisher.
Luc Vander Velpen, for his excellent advice and guidance.

My wife, Griet, who put up with my inattentiveness
during the 18 month project and who painstakingly
reviewed every word, ensuring that the Dutch translation
was faithful to the original English text.

HARLEY LOVEGROVE

TABLE OF CONTENTS

FOREWORD

As far back as I can remember, I have always dreamed of success and riches. Even as a boy I imagined myself as a famous singer-songwriter or the conductor of a classical orchestra, depending upon my mood at the time. For the first 10 years of my career I was bouncing from one great idea to another but without any significant breakthrough. I was earning a living but I had no long-term view of how I was going to make a difference. Luckily, over the years I learned the art of reading people and situations accurately. I figured out who I was, what motivated me and what I was genuinely good at. With regard to my further career, I learned to distinguish between what I enjoyed doing and how I could best earn a living. Around the age of thirty five I truly found myself and I began to build on the experience I had gained over the years. I threw out the surplus and focused on the essential.

The great thing about 'focus' is that it helps you to discover that reality can be a lot more fun than fantasy. I saw that if you take the trouble to understand just who you are and the context in which you find yourself, you can be much more effective at taking decisions. I was still the same person, in the same body, with the same thoughts but I carried far more authority and conviction. I found that people listened more attentively and more readily saw the merits of the plan on offer. I learned that in a grown-up world, where we are playing with real money (someone else's), you only get one chance. Therefore, you should first listen and only act or speak once you fully understand what is required and how to provide it.

By introducing structure into my own career path, I was able to focus on my client's problems much more effectively, because my own personal agenda was so much simpler. People around me were no longer competitors or threats, but opportunities to get me to where I wanted to go - and as long as our goals were the same, there was no harm done.

Over the years I developed the important skill of sharing my vision with others, so they can better understand exactly what I am doing and why. I resolved to take the time to let people see what really needs to be done and, most importantly, how they can play their part. In these last few very successful years, I have concentrated on creating arenas for others to perform in, providing spaces and roles that suit them and in which they are able to excel. This does not mean I have been any less busy and on average I still work more than 12 hours a day, five days a week. I have my clients and continue to work on assignments: how else can you stay in the real picture? The difference is that I have learned to be the conductor of the orchestra instead of trying to play five instruments at once.

I am a naturally busy person, so I tend to lead more than one orchestra at a time. This means that I need to be more selective and to say no more often, both to myself and to others. But today I can honestly say that I am lucky to be one of the minority of people who can genuinely describe themselves as happy. I am content and always look forward to the next day. I have laid down the foundations on which I can enjoy my life, without having to fret over the daily grind that prevents us from doing what we really want.

There is an old adage which says: 'if you want something done, ask a busy person'. It is the nature of all good interim managers to be busy.

HARLEY LOVEGROVE

ABOUT THIS BOOK

Making a Difference is an interim manager's view on how to successfully tackle all kinds of different problems and challenges, even those which at first glance might seem impossible to solve or too risky to take on. Although the book is specifically intended for interim, change and project managers, it is a valuable tool for everyone confronted with a specific task.

The book is divided into two main sections:

Part One contains a nine-step, methodical approach to identifying and tackling a specific problem or challenge.

Part Two covers a wide range of topics, varying from tips and advice on how to hire and fire people, through to all aspects of general management and personal self-development.

For clarity, I have defined an interim manager as someone who has been hired to carry out an assignment that lasts for a predetermined length of time and that has a specific goal or target. Although the term 'interim manager' is sometimes used to describe a manager who temporarily replaces a departmental head (during sick leave or a sabbatical, for example), nowadays the term is used in a much broader context than before, especially when businesses do not want to publicly admit they have a serious problem by advertising for a crisis manager!

Throughout the book I give examples of situations that interim managers are likely to face and I offer pragmatic advice on how to tackle them. To support the book there is an interactive website (www.Making-a-Difference.be) containing a host of additional information and even a reader's feedback blog. There is also a download section offering a wide variety of charts and templates to help set up and manage successful problem-solving projects.

In step two of the nine steps to problem solving, I have posed a classic problem, outlined in the form of a case study, which the reader is invited to solve by posting their own solution on the Making-a-Difference website. By so doing, the reader will not only find my solution to the problem but also the solutions submitted by all the other readers.

For this book I considered three basic aspects of *Making a Difference*:
1. Stepping into a situation that needs improvement - and improving it;
2. Inspiring and coaching those around you to do what they are already doing - but in a more effective way;
3. Adding shareholder value by solving a specific problem that is blocking growth and profitability.

INTRODUCTION

In life we are faced with all different kinds of problems and challenges. Most mature businesses adopt a project methodology for tackling these matters. However, even with a sophisticated project structure, the final 'deliverables' (assuming that we genuinely achieve them) are often disappointing.

Some wise people say that there is no such thing as a problem; there are only opportunities. In my opinion, this is just glib nonsense! Of course, some problems, concerns or worries (call them what you will) are more challenging than others and their solution may provide new opportunities. But a problem is a problem and it needs to be approached and solved in a serious manner.

Typically, interim managers are brought into companies to solve three main kinds of problems:

1. *Recurring problems:* problems that for some reason just keep on coming back, in spite of all best efforts to resolve them (common examples of this type of problem include quality, client satisfaction, personnel issues, disappointing sales or financial results and cash flow difficulties).

2. *Opportunistic problems:* problems that require the taking of hard decisions; 'cross-road' decisions where often there are only two or three options, each with its own complex or even undesirable consequences. These are frequently 'one time-no return' decisions, linked to a problem that can sometimes be considered as a genuine opportunity.

3. *Change problems:* problems linked to the need for a business to change. These may be triggered by the emergence of new competition or by the introduction of new technologies in order to remain competitive, etc... Change problems are usually handled in the form of projects.

Later in the book you will see that nearly all problems (so long as they are not trivial) can be effectively tackled within the framework of a pragmatic, methodical structure. In this way, the results can be measured and assessed clearly.

At the end of an assignment, there are just two possible scenarios: either your client still has a problem or he doesn't; your problem-solving intervention will either have helped him to achieve his objective or it won't have.

Solving one problem often leads to the creation of a whole host of new, unforeseen ones. In this sense, business is a lot like life. In business, however, the unforeseen problems should at least be anticipated and, whenever possible, contained. What I mean by this apparently contradictory statement is that when you start out on a project, it is almost certain that somewhere along the way you will encounter unforeseen issues and side effects. However, if you follow the nine-step approach set out in this book, you will at least know how to tackle them when they arise. In addition, an experienced interim manager should also have at his disposal a network of reliable experts to offer him advice in times of specific need. Being able to identify potential pitfalls and to safely steer one's team away from danger is what is commonly referred to as 'wisdom'.

One thing that an interim manager should never do is to use the excuse 'no one has ever attempted anything like this before' as a reason for unsatisfactory results. Such a statement is almost certain to be untrue. The context for our problem-solving activities may be 'new', but our ideas and plans are not – nor is the essential challenge. If our forefathers managed to build seemingly impossible constructions and govern highly complex societies, we can safely assume that the challenge ahead of us can be resolved, if we approach it in the right way.

In this book I will show you how to step back and observe a business and its problems from a distance. I will offer techniques which will help you to become more objective in your decision making and to create a framework that will allow you and those around you to solve problems in a structured and efficient way. The simple, hands-on method that I propose really does work. It does not require a drastic or implausible personality change. Your colleagues, staff and family may indeed see a change in your approach and perhaps also in your behaviour, but they will be motivated by what they see and will therefore be more willing to become a part of the solution. They will most likely adapt to the new structure you propose, possibly even claiming it as their own.

To get the most out of this book, the reader must keep an open mind; must accept that, however fanciful it might appear at times, *Making a Difference* is based on real life experience and proven success. It is not based on a theoretical model from any single individual, business school or other seat of learning. It offers pragmatic solutions and tried and tested methods, without the complex academic theory that often sounds so impressive but is almost impossible to implement.

Nevertheless, I will suggest further reading and academic study, so that readers will be able to defend their approach in debates without having to rely on this book as their sole reference. The balance between hard core experience and theoretical study is a fine one, and any serious interim manager should set aside time for further self-study at a local business school, or at least for private reading. In order to gain maximum benefit from this book, the reader will need to find his own way of adopting the proposed methodology and to apply the techniques in such a way that the end results are truly his own.

To support the arguments and theories put forward - especially my own - I will often give examples on both a business and a personal level, in order to clarify the point I am making. These personal stories and recollections are printed in grey blocks, so you can skip them if desired.

Management - especially change or project management - is not as easy as it looks. In fact, it is a little like riding a motorcycle: in theory there is not much to it but the reality is very different. Driving fast and straight is easy, but being able to turn tight circles or drive very slowly takes a lot of practice, with the risk that you might fall off a few times. Effective managers get the results they want by steering just the right course, picking up momentum and support along the way.

If you are a young manager or have recently been promoted to a position of authority, you need to accept that you have been selected because the people who pay your wages see potential in you. You may be managing a situation that perhaps you feel has never been tackled before. You will not have much room for manoeuvre and if you make a mistake, everyone will notice. Why? Because when there are problems to be solved, everyone looks to the interim manager to do it, assessing his every move. This book will help you to bridge the gap between learning and experience and will give you insight into how more seasoned managers tackle complex challenges.

In my experience, those who go furthest in life are those who are willing to learn from others. Learning from 'gurus' is fine but I prefer learning from successful predecessors and colleagues, observing their successes and - just as important - their failures.

Winners in business are those who genuinely put their stakeholders or clients first. Winners provide real solutions to real problems, solutions that not only work, but also deliver the results which are actually needed, and not just the results which people think they need. These winners are the people who can really make a difference to a company, providing they have the skills to sufficiently influence their environment, in order to make and maintain the necessary changes. Good interim managers, who are able to shape the business environment and enhance a company's performance, are worth their weight in gold to the shareholders. As such, they are able to negotiate very attractive remuneration packages or daily fees.

Of course, not everything in life is predictable (how boring life would be if it were!). Consequently, an interim manager needs to be adaptable in the face of changing moods, new ideas and challenging propositions. Such managers should not only be able to shape their environment but also – and more importantly - to adapt to the environment in which they find themselves. When things go wrong or if intervention is required, they need to understand which are the right buttons to push - and when they should be pushed. This is only possible if they have anticipated the situation beforehand.

A good interim manager is usually first into the office each morning, planning the day, the week and the month ahead; anticipating the next move once his team members have completed their allotted tasks; contemplating 'what if' scenarios; and preparing responses to questions yet to be posed by those around him.

Similarly, in their private lives good interim managers are often the type of parents who spend more time focusing on what their children actually need, rather than on what they might be asking for. For example, if their child demands ice cream, they would know instinctively that nine times out of ten the child is not really hungry but simply bored and in search of something pleasurable to pass the time. Parents who constantly think ahead of their young offspring will also realise that an interesting activity – which might currently be keeping the kids happily occupied - probably only has a shelf life of twenty minutes. Consequently, they are busy planning the next activity or diversion, well before the children become restless or bored.

PART I

THE NINE-STEP APPROACH
TO PROBLEM SOLVING

I have identified nine fundamental steps for solving serious problems. We will explore each step in detail in the following chapters. Before we start, however, here is a brief overview which will allow us to place each step within its correct functional context:

Step 1: What is the problem?
Understanding and defining the current situation
Step 2: How did the business get to where it is today?
Looking at the past to understand the current situation
Step 3: Cash, culture and competence
Examining your client's foundations
Step 4: What are the aspirations of the business and its managers?
Understanding the long term objectives of the business, to ensure the compatibility of proposed solutions
Step 5: Decision time
Deciding what issues should be tackled first and is the business fully committed?
Step 6: Structuring the solution
Building a solution plan and creating the project
Step 7: Resourcefulness, recruitment and commitment
Ensuring you have the right people, resources and commitment
Step 8: Implementing the solution
Staying on track and keeping focused on the objectives
Step 9: Assessing the results
Measuring success by comparing results with the client's aspirations

The art of problem-solving is to recognize the problems before they become too big to solve and thereafter to use all your resources in new and more efficient ways, in order to create the support which you and the client need. It is for this purpose that the nine-step approach was designed.

Before you embark on the nine steps to solve your client's problems, you must first prepare the 'arena' in which you are going to operate. If you want to succeed, you must understand how and why things went wrong in the first place. To do so, you need to create an environment that will allow your client's management team to clear their heads of routine issues, to think openly and to listen to uncomfortable truths – truths that they may not wish to hear.

For an interim manager this means finding a quiet space on the client's premises, where he can establish his office. I prefer to create a space in which I can have one-to-one meetings in a calm atmosphere. Whatever the available options, it should always be a place where people are temporarily released from their daily pressures. It does not need to be a fancy office, with a kitsch waterfall on the coffee table. On the contrary, I prefer a quiet, uncluttered room with basic furnishings. When I move in at the beginning of an assignment, I always bring my own desk lamp and two easy chairs, and I hang a calming Mark Rothko print on the wall.

Having prepared the working environment and your own frame of mind, you are now ready to proceed to the first of the nine steps.

STEP 1

WHAT IS THE PROBLEM?

UNDERSTANDING AND DEFINING THE CURRENT SITUATION

In order to solve a problem, we must first seek to identify and understand what real issues are at stake. For example, is a worsening cash flow the real problem or is it just the symptom of a poorly performing workforce? Or the wrong product being offered at the wrong price? Or continuing quality faults which have undermined client confidence? Or perhaps the combined effect of all the above?

Start with the symptoms and dig down through all the layers, until you get to the roots of the problem. In life we spend too much time scratching the surface instead of tackling the real issues. Often, this is because the real issues require much more thought and discipline to deal with, especially when there are several causes contributing to the end problem.

A typical example of not understanding the real problem can occur in private life when a couple find themselves arguing about replacing the top on the toothpaste tube. The issue here is not that the toothpaste goes hard and crusty, but the reason why such a minor oversight upsets your partner so much. Do they feel that they are being taken for granted or not appreciated? If you think your problem is just forgetting to put the top back on the tube, then perhaps you need to spend more time understanding who your partner really is and why this seemingly inconsequential matter causes so much frustration.

Similarly, when you find yourself arguing with a colleague about trivia, you can be sure there is some deeper issue which you are both ignoring. Dealing with this kind of situation is never pleasant, but it is something we simply have to do every now and then. The trick is to do it at the right time and in the right place, and in a non-confrontational manner.

In business, a misinterpretation of the real problem frequently occurs when a member of staff leaves to join another company. The most common reason given for leaving is the offer of a higher salary. A higher salary might be the end result of the decision to leave, but what inspired the employee to look elsewhere in the first place? Very few truly contented employees leave for money alone. If they were only dissatisfied with their pay, surely they would have found a way of raising the matter? In over thirty years of business experience I can count on the fingers of one hand the number of people I have known who genuinely left for no other reason than money. A leading US recruitment agency commissioned an in-depth study of why people decide to change employers. This research found that more than 90 percent of people wanted to leave because of conflicts with their colleagues or because of not feeling respected or understood. These were the root causes that led them to shop around for another job; whether the person actually left or not was largely dependent upon how their existing employer handled the situation.

One person's departure is not necessarily a fundamental issue, but this is no longer the case when several leave in a short period of time. The real problem often lays hidden deep within the structure of the business. If your problem today is that your business seems to be losing a high proportion of staff, then you need to look at yesterday's developments to establish the root causes.

But how do we go about finding these root causes in practice? First, we have to determine what the real problem is.

To help answer this key question I recommend you to use Microsoft PowerPoint, because it forces you to think in simple bullet points, without long-winded explanations and excuses. If you prefer not to work with a computer, you can do the same exercise with several sheets of A4 paper and a thick marker pen, to keep you from writing too much text on each sheet.

I. Start by creating a new folder called 'Problems'.
II. Open a new blank presentation with no company templates or fancy backgrounds – this presentation is not intended for showing (unless you like to impress people with your problems).
III. Save this presentation in the folder under the name 'problems *date* V0.1' (make sure you activate the function that automatically places the file name in the footer of each slide).

Tip

I insist that all my colleagues use version numbers, as it can be very dangerous and costly when people start interpreting obsolete data. In addition, there is nothing more frustrating than sitting in a meeting only to be confronted with the idiotic comment 'I think I have a different version from you' and not being able to quickly verify the status.

IV. Do not waste time with presentation formalities; delete the title page and go straight to the slide layout that lets you insert a title at the top and a single list of bullets below it.

V. Type 'Problems' as the title and then add each problem that comes into your head , one problem per bullet. If you go over a single line for a problem, shorten its description until it fits (there will be plenty of time for elaboration later on). A typical 'problems' slide looks like this:

Table 1 • Problems January 2007

- Falling revenues
- Unhappy sales force
- Missed 2006 target
- Can not agree 2007 target
- Production not listening to Marketing
- Marketing Manager too arrogant
- Secretary has resigned
- Jack wants a bigger car

Do not bother about special fonts and layouts - just focus on the words. Do not look for connections or try to group the problems at this stage - just get them down as fast as you can and reward yourself for every one you can think of. If you are lucky, you may only fill one slide. If you are less fortunate, you must keep on going until you cannot think of any more.

VI. Create a new slide for each of the bullets on your 'problems' list. Remember to save your document as you work: now is not the time to lose important information!

VII. Fill each new 'problem' slide with a bullet list of sub-issues for that problem (one bullet per sub-issue, see Figure 2).

Table 2 • Falling revenues

- Lost customer X
- Costumer Y unhappy
- Cheap imports from Bolivia
- No new customers in the last two months
- Pressure to reduce prices
- Service contracts not being renewed
- Big new order promised but not signed!

VIII. Open the slide viewer and arrange the slides into appropriate groups, such as sales, marketing, finance, personnel, etc.. Save this arrangement as 'groups'. Delete duplicates (you will find that annoying issues keep coming back in various guises).

IX. Re-arrange the slides in order of importance and save as 'importance'.

X. Re-arrange the slides in order of logical solution and save as 'logical order'.

XI. Print out your slides and fix them to the wall at eye level.

XII. Ask yourself: 'Have I missed anything? Is there a pattern emerging from problems or sub-issues which appear on more than one slide?' (For example, if you notice that a number of problems relate to human resources, job vacancies, key people leaving the company, complaints about pay, etc., you can link the pattern to a single topic 'staff retention'.)

To gain a broader perspective, first carry out the above exercise on your own; then ask your client to do the same, without letting them see your slides. It is amazing how different the results can be. Sometimes by inviting others to take part in the exercise, you get a much more meaningful result. It is often the company secretary or receptionist who comes up with the most significant insights (these valuable human resources are often overlooked: they see and hear everything, but are trained not to talk about it!).

XIII. Put your colleagues' slides on the wall under your own and once again check for a pattern. This may be the same as yours or it may be a different one.

If the exercise has been successful, you should have gained a good insight into the real issues. These will form the foundation for the next steps. Do not turn the exercise into a public event, but keep it confidential (you will have a chance to involve everyone else later on, when it comes to solving the problems). When you ask someone to carry out the exercise, give them a strict deadline to complete it and commit them to secrecy. If you are not an interim manager but their line manager, and if you do not understand a slide or bullet point, ask them for clarification but refrain from commenting on what they tell you: this might risk shutting the door on possible future insights. Thank them for their input, even if it is painfully inadequate or way off the mark (in your opinion). Go home and reflect on everything you have heard which you did not understand or which you could not agree with.

Whether your client is the CEO of a small business or the manager of a large company, you must help them to accept the fact that a significant share of responsibility for the problem is likely to be theirs. A manager appointed by them who did not perform or a 'good decision turned bad': such matters cannot be blamed exclusively on somebody else. Every boss needs a 'coach', a sounding board – find out who they turn to for advice and talk with them. If your client does not have such a 'coach', find one or suggest yourself.

Managers and CEO's in trouble must be able to swallow their pride and look for people who are better able to cope with the present situation than they are. The interim manager needs to identify and compensate for his client's weakness. If this is not possible, they need to find someone else who can. The CEO or manager needs to be re-assured that there are numerous companies employing experienced interim managers with expertise in the areas where they need help. They must not see this as a personal failure but accept that everyone has their strong and weak points.

In time, we all come to know that being 'the boss' is a lonely and thankless job: when things go right others want to take the credit, but when things go wrong everybody points the finger at them. This is doubly true for an interim manager.

Step 1 is not the time to apportion blame. It is the time to define the real issues, to discard the irrelevant ones and to focus on the important ones. I have seen companies redecorate their reception area in the hope of making a better impression on new investors, while at the same time failing to find sufficient funds to pay the postage for an important promotional mailing.

The following is a true-life example of how one company executive used my suggested method to define his problem.

THE STORY OF THE GLOBAL IT DIRECTOR

The global IT director of an American multi-national company was confronted by his chairman who was looking to substantially reduce costs across the board. The company had been created as a result of a major takeover and developed further over the years through new acquisitions and the sometimes seemingly illogical merging of different departments and divisions. The resulting IT infrastructure was a highly complex network of systems and managers, with a complete lack of integrated data. The equipment was aging and reliability had fallen below acceptable standards. As a result, the IT department was suffering from the soaring cost of user support and the increasing dissatisfaction of the end-users.

Most problems have more than one cause. When these causes are combined, they expose the symptoms of failure and create a need for immediate action. In the global director's case, his IT running costs were too high in comparison with his competitors and his chairman was looking for across-the-board cuts. There was no question of spending additional funds; savings had to come from within existing budgets. The genius of the IT director's insight was not to concentrate on the chairman's demand for reduced costs as the real issue, but to look instead more broadly at the goals of the chairman and of the business itself. By incorporating the Chairman's vision of 'one business, one team', the IT director was able to put forward a powerful case for a substantial technology change project.

Using just three slides, the IT director defined the problem as he saw it. On an additional slide he outlined why change was needed. Instead of stating the problem merely as 'we need to cut ICT costs,' he outlined the requirements of the business as a whole, which in fact reflected precisely the problem of costs and also the bigger issue of communication. He saw the connection and made a logical link. With four slides he was able to communicate clearly to everyone around him both the nature of the problem and the desired outcome.

The text of the IT director's final four slides were as follows:

Business needs
- Communication
- Information
- Collaboration

Personal needs
- Information access
- Speed
- Reliability
- Ease of use

Where do we want it?
- In the office
- At home
- On the road

Why Change?
- Total cost is increasing
- Current environment needs replacing
- Speed is ever more critical
- Users need right tools to remain competitive

These four slides formed the basis for the realization of a global project which fundamentally changed the way in which the employees of the company communicated with each other and even the way in which they worked.

Here is an example of how a practical problem can sometimes turn out to be far more complex than at first sight.

THE STORY OF THE CAR...

Imagine that one morning your car does not start.

Something to consider first: what is your immediate problem? Is it that your car will not start or is it that you might not get to work on time? Remember that you always have choices – if you must be at the office on time, you can always leave your car and find an alternative means of transportation. (Your local video store is full of movies about people who go to the most extraordinary lengths in order to get to somewhere on time). Sadly, in real life we tend to spend our time focusing on the inconvenience and not on alternative solutions.

Back to the car. It is winter and it is very cold outside. You phone the garage and they eventually arrive to fix the problem. They find that the battery is dead and they replace it with a new one. Half an hour later the job is done. You thank them profusely, hand over the cash and everyone is happy. Until a day or so later, when the same problem reoccurs - and this time you are really angry! The emotions you feel are likely to cloud your judgment and you may even do something silly, like phoning another garage!

Let's examine the possible factors influencing this situation:

1. *You have been working late recently, which means driving home in the dark with the fog lights on, the heater on, etc. It has also been raining, so that the wipers were also on. It all adds up to a heavy load on the car battery.*
2. *Because it is winter, you also have to drive to work in the dark, raising the same issues as in point 1.*
3. *Lately you have been so busy that you forgot your car's last routine service check, so that the engine and electrical system are not optimally adjusted.*
4. *Last time you went to the garage you had an argument, because they could not fit you in on the day you wanted. Perhaps this led to a lack of motivation on the garage's part, so that the mechanic did not deliver his usual high-quality service and did not check everything?*

THE NINE-STEP APPROACH TO PROBLEM SOLVING

5. The belt that drives the generator which keeps the battery charged is loose and worn, so that the battery is not being fully charged to cover the increased load.
6. The ignition system is not as efficient as it should be (the spark plugs may be dirty as they were not changed at the last service).
7. The valves on the engine have not been adjusted for a long time because of the lack of a proper service.

These changes in car usage and conditions, combined with the neglect of three crucial components (resulting from the cutting of corners and a de-motivated mechanic) all add up to the car not starting on the morning in question, notwithstanding its new battery.

If the problem had arisen the evening before, it might not have had such an impact, since you would have had time to find an alternative strategy for getting to work and to brief the garage more fully. Who is to blame in this situation - and what can we learn to ensure we avoid a repetition?

SUMMARY

The key lesson of Step 1 is as follows: before any theories are made or any decisions are taken, make sure you get to the real roots of the problem - and then check if others agree with your diagnosis. If you get this first step wrong, you can be sure that all the following steps will also lead you in the wrong direction. However, if you are confident that you understand the problem in its existing form, you are ready for Step 2.

Step 2

How did the business get to where it is today?

LOOKING AT THE PAST TO UNDERSTAND THE CURRENT SITUATION

If the first step to successful problem-solving is to understand exactly what the problem is, the second step is to understand how that problem came about in the first place. As in Step 1, it is all too easy to scratch the surface and to make snap judgments about who is to blame and why. Step 2 is really about understanding past influences and errors.

The expression 'hindsight is a wonderful thing' is mostly used to rebut facile criticism, but like most clichés it also contains a large element of truth. Looking back to see why we took decisions that seemed right at the time; assessing why they subsequently turned out to be wrong; and examining what can be learned from our mistakes: such activities are never a waste of time, providing your trip down memory lane remains focused and objective, and is not simply a search for excuses or scapegoats. Unless we arrive at the correct conclusions, we can be sure that any solution we implement will only be temporary and that the root problem will eventually come back to haunt us.

What are the questions we should ask in order to understand how our client arrived at the position they are in today? As in Step 1, we can use PowerPoint to identify the key issues by asking a series of probing questions about the problem itself (1-12), about the CEO or manager (13) and about the business (14-15):

1. What is the root cause of the problem?
2. What conditions brought it about?
3. Why has it only come to light now?
4. Has this problem (or a similar one) happened before?
5. If so, when?
6. How many times has it occurred?

7. What were the early warning signs that things were starting to go wrong?
8. Were there any similarities in the patterns or conditions prevailing then and now?
9. Is the situation more severe now than the last time it occurred?
10. What did the client do to try to fix it then?
11. Is this solution worth trying again? If so, why? If not, why not?
    a. What did the client overlook or misjudge last time?
    b. Was the approach right but the execution wrong?
    c. What were the early warning signs that the solution was not working?
12. How can we monitor the next solution to ensure that potential failure is detected sooner?
13. Is the client (the management in general or possibly an individual person) partly or solely to blame for the problem?
    a. Are they able to see their own weaknesses?
    b. If not, who is best to coach them and who will they listen to?

If the answer to question 13 is an unequivocal or even a reluctant 'yes', the client must also ask himself the following additional question: 'Can I trust my own judgment this time around?' CEO's and senior management need to take a broader view of past occasions when they have been right and wrong in judging situations and making decisions.

A useful, one-off exercise is to ask them to make a list of their most classic errors of judgment, together with dates and background events. Ask them to try and detect a link or pattern amongst these errors. This will serve to remind them that they are only human and help them to understand in which areas and under what circumstances their judgment is likely to be impaired.

Figure 1 • A typical 'corporate road map'
(usually illustrated with details of products and/or services).

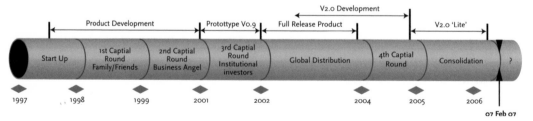

THE NINE-STEP APPROACH TO PROBLEM SOLVING

Many exceptional people have the intuitive ability to know when their own judgment is wrong and when they need to take advice. Others who lack this ability usually only achieve success if they are closely supported by people who can compensate for their weaknesses and who dare to question their judgment, when needed.

14. Has the business deviated from its correct path?
15. If the company has deviated from its path, what has changed and why?

Many of these questions will be difficult to answer, but it is essential that the client should take the time to answer them fully and honestly. Be wary of people who try to kid you that they know all the answers. If they were so clever, they would not be in the mess they are now in! Not all the questions will be relevant in all circumstances but among them are the keys to a number of truths that need to be exposed. Your client's critics can probably point them out immediately, but this does not necessarily mean they are right.

In a time of crisis, the interim manager always finds himself surrounded by people who say 'I told them this would happen' and 'I said this, but nobody listened!' Sometimes these people are right, but often they are not. Either way, they do not add value to the situation because they rarely give constructive advice about how to move forward.

Answering these types of questions is not an easy task for anyone, especially if they are not feeling very positive about the future. Pondering these questions and answers may lead them into a negative emotional spiral. My advice is to ask them to begin alone, but with the reassurance that they have a trusted advisor close at hand.

Keeping your client motivated throughout this tough exercise is extremely important. Make sure that the deadlines are short and follow up on every step. Remain physically nearby: this is not the sort of exercise that can be handled at a distance. You need to be aware of the context and show yourself to be a part of the solution. An interim manager can never *be* the solution; they can only deliver it.

If the problem is brand new - i.e. it has never occurred before or falls outside of the experience of the client – it is important to talk to other people who have had to cope with a similar problem, or who are at least familiar with it. If you can not directly help your client and do not know who these other people are - go and find them!

Many CEO's make the mistake of only relying on the viewpoint of one skill set. For example, if the problem is a cash flow problem, they often only speak with the bank manager. However, the bank manager is exclusively concerned about credit risk and how much he can lend them. Unless the CEO understands the root causes of the problem, a new bank loan in troubled times could be the very worst thing for the company (true, it might enable them to meet short-term commitments, such as next month's payroll, but their overall debt situation will be far worse than it is today). Similarly, if the CEO only speaks about the cash flow problem to the members of his sales team, they will put a different slant on the situation, perhaps convincing the CEO to wait for that big contract they 'know' is just around the corner (overlooking the fact that if the contract ever arrives, it will initially require an additional outlay of funds).

This is why good interim managers only come into their own during their early forties. CEO's need to consult with well-rounded people who have a broad experience of doing business and who have almost certainly confronted problems such as theirs.

In Step 2 you must not confuse the situation by already trying to consider the solution, but instead, you must focus on understanding how your client got into trouble in the first place. Were they spending too much (paying suppliers unrealistic prices) or perhaps too little (not enough advertising)? Were their spending priorities wrong (trying to finish off product development work that could have been completed after an order was placed)?

The following case study is a good exercise for considering the possible causes of a business problem:

David, the CEO of an electrical lighting manufacturer, saw that each year his profi-tability and sales were falling, to the extent that urgent action needed to be taken. He was losing market share at a rate which meant that his business would go bankrupt in less than 18 months. David called his senior managers into his office separately and asked each of them the same question.

First, he asked John, his loyal sales director: 'You've worked with us for fifteen years: why do you think that our results have become steadily worse during the last five years?' The sales manager thought it over and said: 'The problem is that the mar-ket is changing faster than we are – we have been too slow to adapt. Our range of lighting is far too limited. We need more models, more colours. We need to offer our distributors a complete product range, so that they don't look elsewhere. We have to become their sole supplier, so that we don't lose so many deals to outsiders.'

The CEO then called in Peter, the production director, and asked him the same question. Peter replied: 'The problem is that we have been adding more and more products to our range. We now have so many varieties of type and colour that our production costs are running too high, because the production runs are too short and uneconomical. The solution is simple: cut out all the models that are not selling well and reduce the number of colours and varieties for the others. In short, trim down our catalogue and only offer what is economical to manufacture. We may lose some business, but we'll become far more profitable.'

Next the CEO called in his youngest board member. 'Samantha, as marketing direc-tor what do you think we should do to turn around our worsening financial results?' 'That's easy', she answered. 'Go up-market and go direct. We have become too remote; our product range is too narrow and old-fashioned. The production department cripples us by telling us that things can't be done! Our clients know what they want - we just need to offer it to them at a price they are prepared to pay. So what we should do is this: shut down our own production unit, source all the lighting products globally and re-brand them with designer labels endorsed by celebrities. We can keep in touch with our end-clients by opening showrooms in strategic locations, staffed with trendily-dressed lighting consultants, and we can cut out the distributors by selling directly on the Internet.'

Lastly, the CEO spoke with his bank manager, Matthew. He had known him for twenty years and together they had built the business. The bank had provided the loans for starting up the company and had subsequently met their other financing needs, whether for production equipment or new offices. Matthew suggested: 'If I were you David, I would complete the modernization programme we have discussed so often. After all, it's been more than ten years since you last purchased new machinery. The machines you have are no longer as efficient as they could be. Without new equipment, you can never become as cost-efficient as your Asian competitors.'

The CEO went home for the weekend and reviewed the four basic arguments put forward by advisors. Each of them was confident of his or her approach and they had all guaranteed sure-fire results. But which way should he turn? He made a single PowerPoint slide summarizing each of the four key arguments. Much to the annoyance of his wife, he pinned it to the wall beside his bed, so that he could focus on it before going to sleep. He told her that it could mean life or death to the business and that the quality of their retirement years depended on it. Although she wanted to help him, she could only say: 'David, go to sleep. In the morning everything will be much clearer and you will work it all out.' Sure enough, the next morning David woke up and came to a decision.

The CEO's decision can be found on www.making-a-difference.be.
If you would like to offer your own opinion as to the cause of his problem and even suggest a possible solution, please go to the website and you will be eligible to enter the 'Making a Difference' competition. You will also be able to read the author's response, as well as all the other reader's solutions and comments.

A typical example of a repetitive problem faced by many small businesses is their constant struggle with cash flow. This is often the result of under-capitalization. A business which starts off with too little capital may find itself trapped in an endless cycle of cash flow difficulties. Even when sales pick up, they are often hampered by the increased costs of the goods sold. The lack of a financial buffer puts the business under pressure and prevents the full implementation of realistic growth plans.

'The first salesman syndrome' - the complex debate about when to first hire a sales person and the frequently disappointing results which follow this appointment -

comes into play when the business, in an effort to increase revenue, decides to hire a full-time salesperson. The company founders often turn out to be ineffectual sales-people. Even if they are not, there is a prevalent attitude (especially in Europe) that a sales position is somehow inferior to a position as CEO or finance director. I simply do not understand this perception; without sales, there is no revenue; and without revenue, there would be no well-paid jobs for CEO's or financial directors.

I believe that everyone in a company is replaceable (it is often said that the cemetery is full of irreplaceable people), but the value of a good salesman must never be underesti-mated, especially during the infancy of a business. Finding a suitable replacement can take a long time, resulting in a loss of both opportunities and revenue; not to mention the fact that salespeople often take their client base with them when they leave. Ad-mittedly, the arrival of e-business means that there are now companies which are no longer reliant on sales personnel, but they are still very much in the minority.

The key to success is to ensure that the person doing the selling job really enjoys his work and takes pride in it. A half-hearted manager who handles sales because 'somebody has to do it' and who gets upset when a potential client finds fault with his services or products, is not the kind of person you want to send out on the road.

There is a simple reason why seasoned interim managers with a varied background can give more added-value to their clients than their younger colleagues: they have simply witnessed more and have made more mistakes. They have seen companies go bankrupt because they overpaid their suppliers. They have seen mergers fail be-cause no one took account of the difference in cultures. They have seen the problems caused by inflating sales forecasts to keep angry investors happy. They have seen CEO's try to push through changes without gauging the likely level of resistance.

Ultimately, it is from our own past and from the past of others that we can learn the most. In order to survive and prosper, we must avoid repeating the same mistakes. To make a mistake once is unfortunate, twice is careless and three times is criminal! It's as simple as that.

Having examined our client's past influences and established the undetected or un-resolved causes which have brought the business to its current sorry situation, it is now time to look at the basic foundations.

STEP 3

CASH, CULTURE AND COMPETENCE

EXAMINING YOUR CLIENT'S FOUNDATIONS

Knowing your client's foundations will help you to clearly understand the conditions under which any problem-solving project or strategy will be played out. Will it be on a muddy field where every move proves difficult or in the comfort of a floodlit arena, with a crowd cheering you on to victory?

In my definition, the foundations of a business include the following:
- financial position and degree of independence (self-supporting);
- resources (both human & material);
- company culture and history;
- creativity and the ability to respond to stimuli.

Or put more simply: *'cash, culture, and competence'*.

FINANCIAL POSITION AND DEGREE OF INDEPENDENCE

In this section we will examine the extent to which your client's financial position will have an effect on your ability to resolve their problems. Often, when I am facing the managers of a company in trouble (even if they are large, cash-rich organisations), I hear them complain, 'Harley, that's easy for you to say, but we haven't got the resources or the budget. If I had a million dollars and another ten people, life would be easy.'

However, even if they had another million dollars and another ten people, the sad fact of the matter is that in most cases they would still be in exactly the same position six months further down the line, because they are simply unwilling or unable to deal with hard realities head on. Wailing and complaining about the difficulties and injustice of life is much easier than setting out to actually solve the problem (and it also gets you more sympathy).

The first aspect of a business that an interim or crisis manager usually examines (depending on the principle cause of the crisis) is its cash position. They want to know how bad the overall situation really is. A cynic might say they want to see how many man-hours the business can afford to pay them, but I like to believe that it is to determine the time limits and the financial resources available for resolving the crisis. A good interim manager is not interested in throwing cash at problems; they are interested in understanding their root causes and ascertaining the resources they have at their disposal.

It is alarming how many CEO's are ignorant of their real cash flow situation. It is equally alarming how many of them count on landing an improbable sales contract when forecasting their cash flow figures.

Tip

A common error in cash flow planning is to add ill-considered probability figures to the sales forecasts. For example, if a large deal is unlikely to be landed, there is no point in including even a fraction of it in your forecast. It will either all be there or not at all. Similarly, a deal that has only a 50 percent chance of success should not be included for 50% in your revenue estimate. A more accurate method of assessment is to look at the track record of a particular salesperson or sales team in terms of delivering such deals, and then base the revenue forecast on their overall performance - and not on the likelihood of any particular deal coming in. Or to put matters more simply: the deals you are really sure of are in; the deals you are not sure of are out. It is a harsh method but better than working with unreliable probabilities.

Step 3 is the point at which your client must stop dreaming and start looking at the hard realities of the situation. If need be, bring in additional experts to advise you (I often use a brilliant financial auditor who can sniff out even the best hidden agenda). But remember: whatever you discover, sooner or later you will have to confront your client with it, even if it is very bad news. Getting them to face up to the fact that their business has cancer is the first step to dealing with it.

The cash position and forecasted burn-rate provide an estimate of how much time is left. Or in other words, how long your client can survive with the current problem, based on the problem's financial impact per day. This can apply to a complete business or to a departmental budget. In any case, the timeframe and the availability of cash to fund a problem-solving strategy are critical to define the conditions under which a turnaround project will be implemented.

If the business is financially solvent and has no significant cash flow concerns, it can enjoy a level of independence from the human and fixed resources around it. This means that so long as the business generates significant profits, you can leave the existing staff to get on with their daily tasks and bring in additional interim staff to assist in solving the problem or facing the challenge. The ordinary day-to-day operations need not be interrupted. However, in many businesses staffing levels are low and employees are fully occupied with tasks that would normally be carried out by more people. In these circumstances, interrupting their work to ask them to address a serious problem is unlikely to be met with the kind of open and creative thinking that is actually required.

Financial independence (via profits) therefore allows a business to think more broadly, since it does not have to rely exclusively on the efforts of a limited group of overworked people to alleviate the situation.

Contrary to popular belief, however, large and cash-rich businesses do not necessarily have an easier time when it comes to solving their problems for cash. Finding the budget should be easier, but in my experience raising money to solve a particular problem within a large corporation can be more difficult than going direct to banks or private investors. The major corporations all have sophisticated systems to analyse the manner in which you intend to deploy your solution. Complying with their internal audit systems is no easier than convincing a bank manager to increase an already overstretched overdraft facility.

The key when looking at your client's financial foundations is not to consider the re-allocation or borrowing of funds as a solution to the problem at this stage. This should be deferred until to Step 7: 'Recruiting resources and obtaining buy-in'. You should first draw up a detailed plan of exactly what needs to be done, by whom, when, how and (most importantly) why.

Too often businesses allow themselves to get into irreversible debt. This is usually a result of the CEO's willingness to ignore reality and the equally reckless willingness of lending institutions and investors to hand out credit without a basic financial assessment. It is frequently easier to secure a loan for a new executive car than to fund research for new product development. Obtaining loans when they are really needed is always much harder than when they are not. The trick is to negotiate credit limits long before they are actually required and then maintain the discipline to leave them untouched until absolutely necessary.

Most European banks are prepared to lend money to a business as a percentage of the previous financial year's income. This bizarre calculation takes no account of the current situation. If you can give the bank a plausible story, the crisis you are currently facing will be completely overlooked, thanks to your exceptional revenue performance in the past! In this way, many businesses dig themselves into a pit from which they are no longer able to climb out at a later date.

> **Tip**
> *A client can easily bend the truth or play games with their own financial advisors and lenders. Ultimately, however, it is your strategy - the strategy which you, as interim manager, convince them to adopt - which will either solve their problem or make it worse.*

ASSESSING YOUR HUMAN RESOURCES

There is no substitute for wisdom. Even a high dose of intuition and genius cannot be relied upon to solve the problem, without basic experience and an acceptance of the fact that the resulting solution will always be something of a gamble. For this reason, we need to make sure that we surround ourselves with people with more experience and greater insight than ourselves, especially in times of trouble.

Most people overlook or underestimate the resources at their disposal. In the turmoil surrounding their problems, they forget about the stranger they once met on a train, who said that he knew a really good salesperson; or the former boss who told them: 'If I can ever be of assistance, you only need to ask.' Or perhaps they are too stubborn to ask for help until it is much too late.

The challenge in Step 3 is not to allocate people to tasks, but simply to assess their potential value:

- What are their real skills?
- Are they capable of more than they are currently credited for?
- What is their availability?
- Are they in a position to think about the problem clearly?

- How motivated are they to help?
- Is their agenda the same as ours? (Just because we want the problem solved does not necessarily mean that they do).
  If not,
- What incentives, financial or otherwise, can be offered to rally them to the cause?

Experienced interim managers usually take time early on in an assignment to interview all the company's key personnel. This not only allows them to understand the level of skills and resources available, but also gives them a wide diversity of views with regard to the current situation and helps them to identify the dominant coalition within the business structure. Experience shows that the person who delivers the initial briefing may have a biased perspective and is often incapable of reading the real situation.

Knowing your client's needs and enhancing their resources by mining the store of knowledge in your network database are two of the most important ingredients for success. It is equally important to remember that everyone in your network also has a network of their own - and these contacts, in turn, also have further networks. When people say 'it's a small world', they are only speaking the truth. For most of us in business, access to the right person is probably no more than three to four networks away. Or, as you get older, perhaps as few as one or two.

Figure 2 • The inter-linking of personal networks.

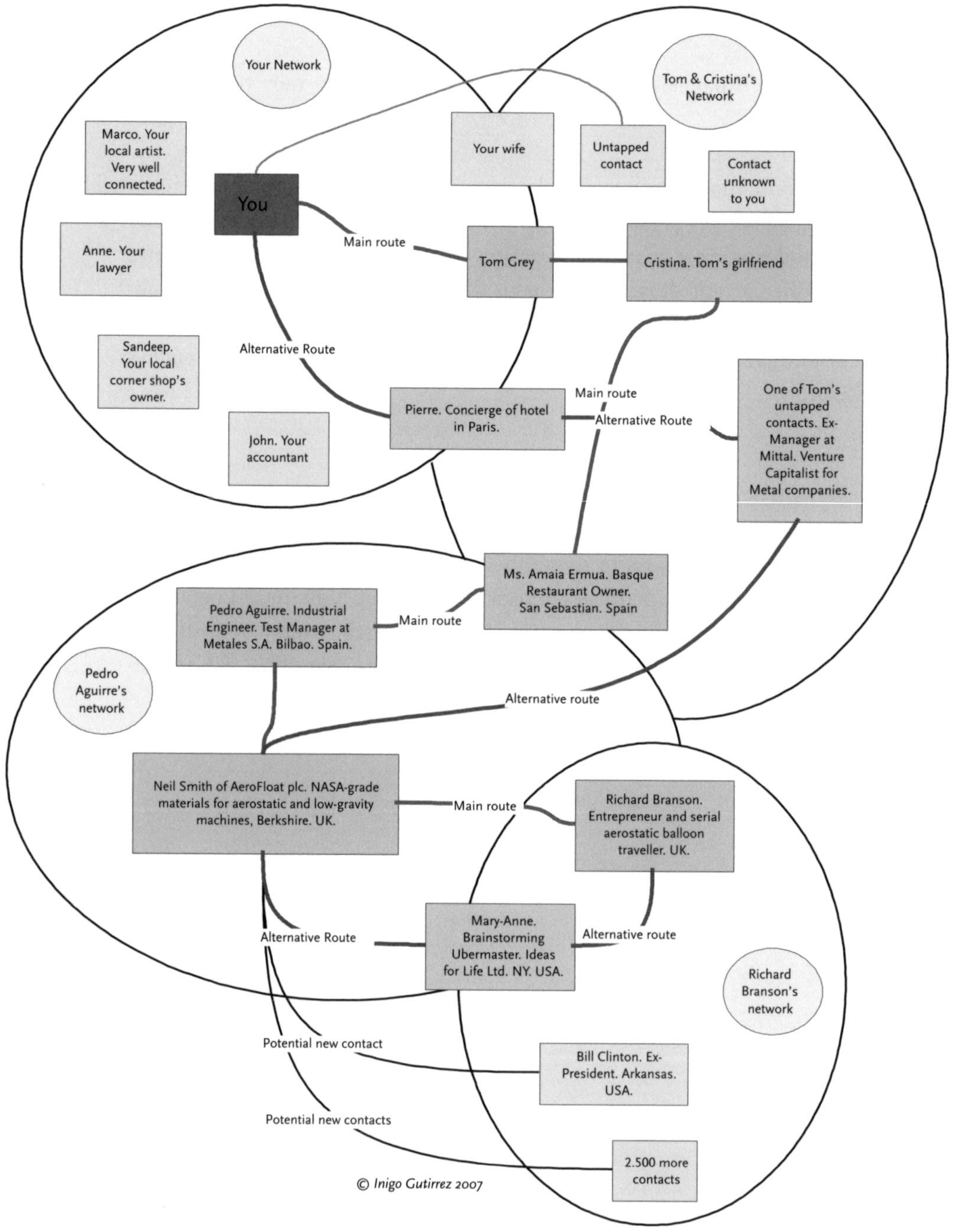

Your Network

Tom & Cristina's Network

Marco. Your local artist. Very well connected.

Your wife

Untapped contact

Contact unknown to you

You

Anne. Your lawyer

Main route

Tom Grey

Cristina. Tom's girlfriend

Alternative Route

Sandeep. Your local corner shop's owner.

Pierre. Concierge of hotel in Paris.

Main route

Alternative Route

One of Tom's untapped contacts. Ex-Manager at Mittal. Venture Capitalist for Metal companies.

John. Your accountant

Ms. Amaia Ermua. Basque Restaurant Owner. San Sebastian. Spain

Pedro Aguirre. Industrial Engineer. Test Manager at Metales S.A. Bilbao. Spain.

Main route

Pedro Aguirre's network

Alternative route

Neil Smith of AeroFloat plc. NASA-grade materials for aerostatic and low-gravity machines, Berkshire. UK.

Main route

Richard Branson. Entrepreneur and serial aerostatic balloon traveller. UK.

Alternative Route

Mary-Anne. Brainstorming Ubermaster. Ideas for Life Ltd. NY. USA.

Alternative route

Richard Branson's network

Potential new contact

Bill Clinton. Ex-President. Arkansas. USA.

Potential new contacts

© Inigo Gutirrez 2007

2.500 more contacts

THE NINE-STEP APPROACH TO PROBLEM SOLVING

In this *fictional* diagram (Figure 8), you can see that Richard Branson is within 3 networks' reach of your own!

Route One:

1. Firstly, you contact Tom, who - having been invited to every party in college - knows more people than the Dalai Lama.
2. He quickly puts you in touch with his girlfriend, Cristina, who is based in her bank's Madrid office.
3. She contacts Amaia, the owner-chef of a fashionable restaurant in San Sebastian, where many businessmen stop off between deals, including anybody who is anybody in the aeronautics industry - an area of business close to Richard Branson's heart.
4. From Amaia, you are sent to Pedro Aguirre, an old client at Amaia's restaurant, who sells futuristic alloys and who has Airbus as one of his most important clients, just across the border.
5. One of Pedro's other clients, Neil Smith, is a merchant in top-quality materials for the transport industry: yachts, private jets, speed boats and stratospheric balloons for the Met Office. Coincidentally, he is also a purveyor of specialist balloon frames, including Richard Branson's own.
   Your connection with Richard Branson is made.

Alternative Route:

1. Tom suggested the hotel in Paris for your wedding anniversary, where Pierre - the concierge - has probably seen more VIPs than the Queen of England.
2. Pierre quickly puts you in contact with an ex-manager of Mittal, from whom he got a large tip when he met those Russians with their underdeveloped nickel mine in Siberia.
3. This venture-capitalist is eager to help (as are most people, with the right incentive), since he has approached Richard Branson on a number of occasions (albeit indirectly).
4. His link is Neil Smith, who advises Richard Branson on the structural stress of materials for his aeronautical voyages, via one of Branson's own advisers, Mary-Anne.

In business, acquaintances (some call them friends) are the most precious resource you can have. Look closely at your network database. How many of them can you consider as acquaintances or friends? How many would be willing to help you out, in one way or another, if you needed it? How many could put in a good word for you with a potential client? How many could put you in touch with really good advisors, should you need specialist help? How many would lend you cash, if required? How many would you invite to your daughter's wedding? Friends need nurturing: it is important to keep the friendship alive, especially if it is also beneficial to your career or business. This obviously involves a degree of socialising, but it is important to maintain the right balance between family and work. Sometimes, the interim manager needs to remind the client to focus more closely on their own networks and to look at them from a completely new angle.

THE STORY OF THE CLIENT AND THE SUPPLIER

Today, the fine line between client and supplier is becoming finer all the time. I once ran a multi-million euro project and during its implementation I met numerous sales representatives and technologists from large multinational suppliers. Of course, these people were selected by their companies specifically to support ventures such as the one I was undertaking on behalf of my client. However, by the end of the project they wanted to know where I was going next and I was also interested to find out what opportunities they had in the pipeline with other clients. They were aware of all the big new investment plans, knew all the right people to contact and could recommend me as a specialist. As long as no transfer of cash or corruption takes place, this is a system which benefits everyone.

When assessing resources, we need to take a fresh look at all the people available to us and at their true potential. This includes all the people they, in turn, know, who might be able to help us in one way or another. For example, it can be very useful for a local business to make contact with an experienced photocopier salesman, since he will know which companies in the area are growing, which are in trouble, which are moving to bigger offices, etc.

'Physician, heal thyself'. This quote from the New Testament has proven its wisdom time and time again. I am often astonished how people fail to identify the solutions to problems close to home, when they are able to spot them easily in other organisations. The simple fact of the matter is that an interim manager can often see the real issues more clearly, because he is able to stand at a distance, thereby gaining perspective. When a client confronts an interim manager with a problem, it is the client's anxiety and lack of perspective that prevents him from thinking freely; the emotional side of the brain takes over and rationality goes out the window. If foot soldiers were always rational, there would be no heroes. On the other hand, if officers were not rational, the supply of foot soldiers would be depleted very quickly!

The CEO does not run the business on his own. He is assisted by numerous colleagues and it is understandable that these colleagues also respond emotionally to the confrontation of important issues. This means that they cannot always be relied upon to analyse the situation any more objectively than the CEO. Only employees and consultants who are not emotionally involved have a chance of seeing the real situation. This explains why it is often the people we least expect who confront us with the most obvious truths.

We can draw similar conclusions if we observe ordinary people in stressful situations, such as a live interview or a television quiz show, where everyone can see them make a fool of themselves. These people normally have to pass a series of preliminary selection rounds before they can appear, so how do we account for the fact that their otherwise quick and nimble brains suddenly become so slow and muddled? Even the simplest questions, posed under stressful conditions, can raise all manner of ridiculous answers from otherwise intelligent, well-educated people.

By observing people, you can discover a great deal about their characters and their surroundings.

THE STORY OF THE OFFICE CLEARNER

I once knew a cleaner who filled the Perrier water bottles in the boardroom with tap water, but no one challenged her because they didn't want to upset her. Her reason *for doing this was not to save money, but because the boardroom was on the 7th floor and the crates of water were too heavy for her to carry. So she took it upon herself to solve the problem in her own way, filling the bottles from a tap in the boardroom kitchen. It is implausible to think that no one noticed, but on the other hand no one complained either!*

When I am on interim management assignments I often talk with the cleaners: I am impressed by how much insight they can have.

THE STORY OF THE UNTIDY OFFICES

Once I was working as a stand-in COO, desperately trying to save a sinking company from going under. One night when I was working late the cleaner came into my office, smiling away and enquiring why I was still here. I asked her if she was worried about the situation. She told me: 'Listen dearie, I have been cleaning this building for the last twenty years. I have seen all sorts of companies and managers come and go. One day I'll be cleaning someone else's desk, if you don't mind me being so bold. When the current lot came in, I never saw such a mess. You would have thought that everyone had won the pools, the way they were all carrying on! Fancy cars, late night parties, leaving a filthy mess.' 'Parties?' I asked. 'They called them brainstorming meetings. They looked like parties to me, but what do I know? The more mess they make, the more overtime I get. So don't get me wrong - I ain't complaining. It's just their la-di-da attitude that gets up my nose'.

This short exchange told me everything I needed to know. It reminded me that I, too, was trying to clean up the 'mess' caused by three years of excessive, uncontrolled and undirected expenditure and the flagrant wasting of hard-earned shareholder's money. It was a discouraging assignment and it forced me to face the depressing reality that it is hard to turn around a business which has earned a reputation for extravagant behaviour and excessive spending.

Silly as it may seem, a problem may sometimes strike us as being so unexpected and so intractable that we often fail to look in the most obvious place for a solution. When a husband asks his wife: 'Have you seen my keys darling?' the answer is logical and straightforward: 'Have you looked on the key rack, dear?' Incredible but true. At that moment we see our problem as being so complex that we discount the obvious solution, even when it is staring us in the face.

REPEATED FAILURE AND A LACK OF RESOURCES

When I am brought in by a company to help solve a recurring problem, the most common reason given for the said problem is 'a lack of resources'. However, clients rarely accept that their problems are recurring. Mostly, they try to pretend that the problem is 'new', in order to get around the embarrassment of coming to terms with repeated failure. Irrespective of whether the client is a small family business or a division of a multinational corporation, the 'lack of resources' excuse is often used but rarely true. When a CEO or manager thinks that their problem is caused by a lack of human resources, don't encourage them to bet on it - because it is almost certain that they will lose!

It is true that over the last 20 years many businesses and public institutions have undergone radical headcount reductions, in order to sustain the continual drive for increased efficiency and to satisfy the competitive pressure to cut labour costs by increased automation. Even so, the 'lack of resources' debate is often little more than a mask designed to conceal genuine inefficiency or a lack of creativity and insight. I do not wish to debate the morality of this practice, but simply to show that an interim manager should never underestimate the psychological impact that a headcount reduction can have on the remaining employees.

If you travel to any country where there are low wages and high unemployment, you will immediately notice much lower levels of efficiency. A business trip to China will quickly reveal that away from the modern business complexes, large groups of people are still working the land by hand without basic motorized tools. Where the workforce is so cheap and plentiful, such labour-saving equipment is simply not needed - or even desirable. Consequently, it is important that every criticism of efficiency should be viewed within the context of the situation and not necessarily compared with an 'ideal' norm.

It is imperative that we find ways of maximising the resources available to us. Not by overburdening our best employees to the extent that they cease to be productive, nor by making excuses for the less effective ones. A poorly deployed or trained member of staff is a serious misuse of resources and skills. Later in the book we will address in detail the problem of ensuring that people are allocated to the positions where they will perform best. For now, it is more important to understand exactly what human resources you have at your disposal.

A simple and effective method is to build up a simple human resource table, like the one shown below, by listing the names in the left column, adding a few keywords to characterize each person as a resource in the middle column and indicating their availability in the right column.

Table 3 • Human Resources

NAME	RESOURCE	AVAILABILITY
John Doe	Clear thinking, little action	Yes
Ivan Sanchez	Cash (100K-750 Euros)	Maybe
Celine Jones	Always has a critical word	Yes
Frank Townsend	Brilliant SW engineer	In 5 weeks
Paul Miles	Excellent project manager	Yes
Fiona Smets	Tri-lingual project coordinator	Yes 50%
Brian de Silva	Motivator & team leader	Yes 80%
Petra Deklerck	Graphic designer & web builder	Yes
etc. etc.		

Such a table is useful when you are selecting a team and also for ensuring that you do not have a duplication or gap in skills. Sometimes I even write the names on one side of a small card, with a brief overview of their skill sets on the other side. By simply moving the name cards around on top of a large desk, one can start to see the beginnings of an organizational chart and the potential areas of shortfall.

Because the interim manager is independent and has an external view of matters, he is often best placed for the task of optimizing the effective use of the human resources. Unfortunately, most people are simply not good at seeing the potential which is often sitting right in front of them.

Experienced interim managers are used to making quick assessments, in order to decide on the suitability of personnel for a particular project. However, at this stage we are not yet really concerned with the allocation of particular staff to solve particular problems, but are more interested in creating a mini-audit of the value of the human resources available to us. This exercise is not an investigation into existing job efficiency, but more an inventory of the skills demonstrated by the staff in their work, with special emphasis on skills and ambitions which are still hidden, waiting to be given a chance. It is extremely important that the staff under scrutiny should also see matters in this light. It should not be perceived as a head count.

When assessing your resources to see if they are sufficient to solve a particular problem, don't be afraid to ask for help. I have lost count of the number of times I have heard employees and the friends of company directors say: 'If only he had asked, I could have helped!' Remember that pride is the enemy of invention. Musicians tend to produce their worst music when they decide to make a solo album, writing the songs and playing all the instruments themselves. The absence of creative conflicts and an inflated belief in their own worth destroy objectivity and diminish critical perspective and inspiration. Even the most talented artist needs a producer and in times of difficulty every manager or CEO needs the support of people who can offer challenging advice from a basis of knowledge, wisdom and insight.

COMPANY CULTURE, HISTORY AND VALUES

Company culture plays a role in determining the approach towards the solving of complex problems and, as a result, also has an impact on the solution itself. The culture of a company is often evident in their value and/or mission statement. For example, Walt Disney's value statement is:

- No cynicism ;
- nurturing and promulgation of 'wholesome American values' ;
- creativity, dreams and imagination ;
- fanatical attention to consistency and detail ;
- preservation and control of the Disney 'magic'.

If your client does not have a value statement, it is a worthwhile exercise to ask them to write down what they think the company's most important values are. If they do have a value statement, see if it is consistent with what is published on the website and in other in-house publications. The interim manager should also carry out his own comparison exercise, matching his own assessment of the reality of the situation with the perception of the management team.

For genuine problem-solving, only values which are perceived to be authentic should be considered. If the client company's internal values are different from its publicly stated ones, the interim manager should only take into account the internal ones. Moreover, he must seriously consider either trying to change the internal ones (reality) to match the external ones (fantasy) or, if it is preferable, vice versa.

If employees see contradictory values on their company's website, they lose respect for their leadership team. Worse, they come to believe that there is difference between what the leadership team claim and what is true. This in turn can create an unpleasant and cynical culture that is hard to change.

An extreme example of contradictory values can be when there is hypocrisy within a company towards gender equality, race or disability. For example, if it is believed that a member of staff has discriminated against another member of staff and the middle management has done nothing about it, the situation can escalate very quickly unless a senior manager steps in. In this case, it is imperative that the law is followed and that common decency prevails. The standards the CEO and the leadership team set, and the rules they choose to follow, are a matter of personal choice and company policy. However, their attitudes and practice, over a period of time, form the company culture - and this culture is something of which all the staff should be proud. For this reason, it is important to keep the culture consistent and true. The interim manager needs to take full account of the actual culture. If it needs changing, it needs to be seen to change from the top downwards, with bright and clear statements, followed up by practical action.

CONSIDERING CULTURE AND ITS INFLUENCE ON CHANGE

Culture is not only about values and ethos. Company culture can be regarded as the company's DNA, formed early on at the very birth of the business. Like a string of genes, a healthy culture will enable the business to reproduce itself far more efficiently than a poor one.

A large multinational, built up over the years via aggressive mergers and acquisitions, followed by rounds of asset stripping and regrouping, is likely to have a culture based on uncertainty and change. In fact, it is likely to have multiple sub-cultures, making it extremely difficult to manage on a global level. On the other hand, a small to medium-sized family-owned business, with a stubborn, narrow-minded CEO, is unlikely to move far from its starting position, and its employees will always know where they stand and what to expect.

A company with a free-thinking culture of innovation may be in a state of almost constant change, making the business difficult to control. The company's employees may feel insecure, thereby making it difficult to implement even a basic strategy. If the company is profitable and change is the core of its success, expanding the business will always be difficult without creating separate operational units.

Change management in a small company is normally much easier than in a large one, especially if the team is young, open-minded and relatively inexperienced. Changing the way people work or behave in a large, mature, corporation is a very different matter. The levels of political resistance, lobbying and general apathy can be much higher. The decision-making process is often cumbersome and slow, and frequently there are the hidden agendas so well concealed that you only discover them when it is too late. For this reason, it is vitally important to know just how long your client is prepared to tolerate the current situation and therefore how hard you will need to apply change over a given period of time.

In our private lives, at the beginning of personal relationships, we concentrate on looking for similarities: hobbies, food, music, sports, travel destinations, etc. Only later do we realize that strong relationships are built upon complementary differences. The similarities may, in fact, become areas of potential conflict. Over time, especially when the relationship is augmented with children, a family culture begins to form. It can be based around rules, but more often than not it is based on fundamental beliefs.

In business, these beliefs will either be a hindrance or a help in tackling issues and implementing change-related projects.

Usually, a dominant person within the company (often the CEO or the founder) forms a coalition around himself. The resulting ethics, vision and culture are largely born from the first formation of this group (the founder typically seeks out like-minded people, even though he probably won't admit it!) and from there the recruitment process begins. The employees who are appointed at the beginning of the company's existence will, to a large extent, collectively formulate the company ethic.

In fast-growing companies, it is common to hear employees say: 'the company has changed, it's not like it used to be.' This is unavoidable; growth does change the working environment: the CEO who used to pop into everyone's office is now at the end of a corridor on the top floor and barely remembers his colleagues' names. But the root culture remains the same. This explains why mergers between two apparently similar businesses with compatible products and markets can often result in disappointing performance for the first months or even years – and it is the clash of culture that frequently forms the biggest problem.

A good interim manager should be able to adapt quickly to different cultures and must be able to use all his tricks and skills to achieve results in whatever cultural environment he finds himself.

A useful way to compare cultures within a company is to look at their meeting policies: how often are they held, how easy are they to set up, how long do they last, do they always have objectives, agendas and minutes with action points, etc.? Another way is to compare the allocation of mobile phones. What rules are applied to the selection and distribution? How are the invoices paid? Can senior managers, who only use them for a few minutes per day, have a better quality model than the sales personnel, who use them all day? Such matters reveal a great deal about the company culture.

The level of difficulty/complexity for the solving of a particular problem is often directly related to the level of openness for change within the company culture. And this openness is greatly influenced by circumstance and habit.

Try the simple act of giving away cash in a busy high street and you will be amazed how hard it actually is! Try next to imagine why this might be and apply the same reasoning to the implementation of even the smallest change in a business. What seems like a real 'bargain' to you - an offer that the employees will love - may provoke the hardest possible resistance.

For example, if you replace somebody's two-page per minute desktop printer with a 30-page per minute multifunctional unit, you might reasonably expect this change to be welcomed. Yet in spite of all the obvious advantages of the new fast and flexible machine, you will often find that the simple effort of having to get off a chair and walk across the room to the floor standing model will be met with great resistance by the users, particularly if they feel that the new unit is no longer 'theirs'. Taking away anything, no matter how useless, is very difficult, especially if it is replaced by something that no longer 'belongs' to the person who had to 'give up' the discarded unit.

The key to controlling 'resistance to change' is communication: getting your message across. Why are we doing this? Who is endorsing it? What are the benefits? Why there is no need to be afraid, etc.

The golden rule is to keep things relatively 'close to your chest' until you have fully explored the issues yourself. Any other approach might be interpreted as brashness or even laziness. You have to work out the details first - only then should you share them with others.

To summarise: before attempting to solve your client's problem, look closely at their root culture. How might this culture be an asset or a hindrance in tackling the issue? How can you best play your cards in order to achieve maximum results in the most efficient way? At some point, communication will become the key. Will you go for complete openness with everyone or will you decide to keep things close to your chest, only sharing what people need to know? How will the internal politics of the business influence your decision-making (especially when it comes to the deployment of resources)? To what extent will you need to consider (especially for publicly listed companies) the impact that your decision will have on the shareholders and the outside world?

STEP 4

WHAT ARE THE ASPIRATIONS OF THE BUSINESS AND ITS MANAGERS?

UNDERSTANDING THE LONG TERM OBJECTIVES OF THE BUSINESS,
TO ENSURE THE COMPATIBILITY OF PROPOSED SOLUTIONS

Everybody's going somewhere
Riding just as fast as they can ride
I guess they've got a lot to do
Before they can rest assured
Their lives are justified
JACKSON BROWNE

In life, it helps if you are able to decide at an early stage precisely what it is that justifies your existence - no matter how futile it might seem! It is always reassuring to meet someone who knows who they are, what it is they want to do and why they want to do it, even if they do not know how.

Similarly in business, if your client knows what his core business is, who his clients are and why they choose his company over the competitors, it is likely that they will be able to face any problems which arise with maturity and wisdom. However, your client will also need to know what long-term aspirations they have for their business and (more or less) how they intend to achieve them. Some companies manage to include these matters in their mission statement; others do not. Those that do, find it much easier to communicate and to do effective business with others.

An American salesman I once worked with used to quote Wayne Gretsky, the famous Canadian ice hockey player: 'I skate where the puck is going to, not where it has been.' This piece of sporting wisdom has stuck in my head like a mantra. When I first heard it, it encouraged me to ensure that my business concerns were going in the direction of the market and not off at some idiosyncratic tangent.

There are far too many people who spend their lives rushing around 'being busy', but who never seem to progress. Mostly, this is because they never take the time to assess exactly what it is they are doing - and why. If you walk around looking at the ground just in front of your feet, you will have far more accidents than someone who has trained himself to keep his head up, looking further down the road. Not only do they know where they are heading, they can see potential hazards much earlier and react accordingly. It is just the same with businesses: they need to keep focused on the horizon but not ignore the hazards in front of them. This is not always an easy balance to strike.

In many ways, Step 4 is the most straightforward of the nine steps you have to take. Put simply, it requires you to understand exactly what your client wants to achieve on a personal level and also what his ambitions are for his business. These aspirations should not be considered as short term, because they actually represent 'the end destination'. The task of the interim manager is to remove any obstacles which may be blocking the current path, thereby preventing their eventual realization.

Here are some typical aspiration-type questions which an interim manager needs to ask his client (to be adapted according to the circumstances):

1. If I were to ask you what you hope you and/or your company will have achieved in five or ten years time and how much money you will be making, what would your answer be? More importantly, why?
2. How will you know when you and/or your business have become 'successful'; whether or not you have realised your aspirations? What are your key indicators for measuring this success?

If you know the direction in which your client's company is going and if you are also able to quantify its success (or failure), then you should be able to anticipate the challenges ahead. If your client does not have either a personal and/or a business mission statement, they cannot have a road map. And without such a road map, they can never explain where it is they want to take their company or even how they intend to get there.

Step 4 is therefore the moment to review your client's existing mission statement or even to write a new one.

If your client does not know where he is going, how can he ever expect his staff and investors to know? When such companies encounter problems, they are much harder to solve. The right decision, the right choice will always be harder to find, since the lack of a clear objective makes all options seem possible. They will be more afraid of making the wrong decision and will consequently forget to focus on the right one. It is for this reason that a road map should be created, if one does not exist already. The road map will need to be discussed with the management team and must take account of their feedback. Key indicators of success will need to be defined and a realistic timeline for the achievement of objectives will need to be set, if the road map or mission statement specifies certain goals or targets.

Figure 3 • Company road map

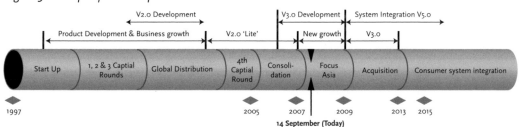

From now on, every decision your client takes should fit within the framework of their global mission statement. Every step they take should be in the direction outlined in their roadmap. The mission statement and the roadmap must be embedded into the consciousness of the entire workforce and reflected in all its internal communications.

A good mission statement is one that can easily be understood by everyone and expresses the real ambitions of the CEO and his shareholders.

The Story of THE MISSION STATEMENT

Here are some typical one-line corporate mission statements. Note how easy they are to understand and to communicate to others:

Boeing (1950): 'Become the dominant player in commercial aviation and bring the world into the jet age'

Ford Motor Company (early 1900's): 'Ford will democratize the automobile'

Microsoft (circa 1989): 'A computer on every desk and in every home'

Sony (early 1950's): 'Become the company best known for changing the worldwide poor-quality image of Japanese products'

Wal-Mart (1990): 'Become a $125 billion company by the year 2000'

Walt Disney: 'To make people happy'

I also like to encourage everyone to have their own personal mission statement. They should also be equally straightforward. For example, at the time of writing, mine is threefold:

- *To enjoy my work and be happy in my private life (finding an equilibrium that allows both)*
- *To establish a financial base that allows me to remain comfortable*
- *To be generous in nature and in deed.*

Every decision I make is made with this trinity of objectives in mind. As mission statements go, it is not as concrete as Wal-Mart's, but then again I am the only person it affects. My values are only important to me and my general well-being. I do not need to communicate my personal mission statement to others, but if someone else happens to read it, they should be able to recognise me within it; it should not appear at odds with my character or situation.

THE NINE-STEP APPROACH TO PROBLEM SOLVING

Many people complain that writing a personal mission statement is difficult. For these people, I suggest breaking the statement down on a year by year basis. I do this by asking them the following question: 'If you were run over by a bus on the way home from work, what three things would your boss most miss about you?' (I do not mean personal attributes, like a sense of humour or comradeship, but hard, professional qualities). For example, a boss might say of a secretary:

1. 'Who is going to organize all the departmental meetings and events?'
2. 'Who will I be able to consult about the genuine mood of my staff?'
3. 'Who will fetch my laundry and run my other errands?'

The secretary might be happy with the first two comments but not necessarily with the third one! In this case, she needs to decide on what three questions she would like to hear at the end of the following year and convert them into her mission statement. For instance:

'To be seen as a hard working and reliable secretary, who is especially appreciated for her deep insight into the moods and aspirations of her colleagues; who is an exceptional organizer of both large and small scale events; and who is the primary source for accurate departmental reporting and results analysis'.

Whether or not it can be attributed to the lack of a mission statement or a clear company roadmap, it remains a common fact that too many companies allow themselves to be steered off their intended course by supposedly good 'opportunities'. At first, this might not seem to be a major problem, until one day the company discovers that its mighty flagship has been replaced by a flotilla of rowboats, all rowing off in different directions. In the 1990's this phenomenon was commonly known as 'business unit divergence'.

In the mid-nineties many companies allowed their clever, career-minded employees to 'develop' their own business ideas within the framework of the existing core business. Five years later, most of these companies ended up with multiple CEO's (often with the meaningless title of 'Business Unit Manager'). With little or no shared services, they also created proportionally high overheads, when compared with their more focused competitors. Eventually, most of them lost their corporate identity and were forced to rapidly re-structure on their 'core' businesses. This is not a new phenomenon and is not restricted to large corporate organisations. It has been going on since the beginning of time, ever since the first children started to have differing dreams from their parents.

But even if our clients have their aspirations summarized in a strong mission statement and mapped out on a clear roadmap, it can still be interesting to look at the relationship between aspirations and disappointment in the short term.

If you have ever been shopping and returned home delighted with your purchases, only to become disenchanted soon afterwards, it may well be that your aspirations were not thought through or were wildly optimistic. Perhaps you were just unlucky and purchased a faulty product. On the other hand, if you find this a repetitive symptom (either in products, services or personnel), you need to consider your aspirational objectives (expectations) more seriously before parting with your money. An example:

THE STORY OF A LAWN MOWER

1. *If your first objective is to find a way to cut grass more quickly, the colour of the lawn mower should be irrelevant.*
2. *If your second objective is to use as little storage space as possible, a long list of accessories is superfluous.*
3. *If you need to lift the mower up flights of steps, its weight is a significant factor but not the type of fuel it burns.*
4. *If you are likely to buy the large plot of ground behind your house, you may need to consider how long you are likely to want to keep the machine; if it only needs to last three years, the quality of its construction will not be so important.(you cut the grass ten times a year for three years, which means it only needs to last through thirty mowing sessions - perhaps you can even do this without getting it serviced!).*
5. *If you regard the act of cutting the grass as an exercise to keep fit, perhaps the power of the engine is less important.*
6. *If money is no object, you should consider buying a bicycle and paying someone else to cut the grass (you'll have more fun, keep fit - and the bike takes up less space in the garage).*

In reality, once we have set our minds on a new lawn mower, our aspirational thinking tends to be forgotten and we find ourselves considering all kinds of irrelevant data during the salesman's pitch: will the machine impress our family and friends, is there something distinctive about it that will make us special?. Once we 'desire' the mower sufficiently, we can easily convince ourselves that we have bought just the right machine for the job and the bargain of a lifetime.

Everyone knows that advertisements are created to solve our problems, even when we are not aware that we have any! They trick us into buying things which we might not otherwise have purchased. The soap industry tempts us with creams and lotions to keep our skin clean, young and fresh looking; yet we know that essentially soap is soap. If every 'new and improved' detergent were truly better than the previous version (as the advertisers always claim), how on earth did anyone ever manage to get their clothes clean twenty years ago?

When everything seems to be going well with a business, it might seem a waste of time to consider its aspirations and long-term objectives. However, if the company has a serious problem and does not know where it is going, it is highly unlikely that a satisfactory solution to the problem will ever be found. Similarly, on a personal level, a doctor might prescribe an exercise routine to satisfy your needs, but it will not help you to get fit, unless you understand what it is you actually want and why. An anti-depressant tablet can help you to feel less bad, but only an improvement in your overall circumstances is likely to make you feel happier in yourself. And happiness can only be achieved if we know what we really want and if we believe that we can obtain it.

Tip

One of my golden rules is: before you set out to do something, always have a clear idea of the result you want to achieve. This rule can even be applied to something as mundane as a phone call. Before I pick up the handset, I make a mental note of the result I expect to obtain from the call. For example, when I make a phone call to an important new business contact with the aim of obtaining an appointment to meet him, I make a mini-plan of the benefits of such a meeting, ensuring that they flow smoothly off my tongue and that they make sense from his point of view. If I have the appointment when the call ends, then my mission has been successful. It is often a mistake to try and drag out the call once its original objective has been achieved, even if the person on the other end of the line seems interested. Leave what you are saying for the meeting. After all, you have just persuaded your contact that your mutual interests can best be served by meeting face to face, rather than by talking over the phone.

It is a good idea to ask your client why he has certain aspirations. If his motivations are weak, there is a good chance that the aspiration will be quickly discarded. For example, your client may want to be the number one supplier of vacuum cleaners in Romania. In itself, there is nothing wrong with this. But the client needs to understand exactly why he wants to achieve this goal. The interim manager needs to challenge the client's perception of himself, in order to make sure this perception is in line with the client's real ambitions and desires - and is not simply the ego of the CEO talking. So often CEO's get themselves – and their companies - into difficulty because they are living up to someone else's expectations and have not yet formed their own.

The aspirations of CEO's are often seen by others as being mad or arrogant: according to some, they have 'big dreams' and even bigger heads. But if a CEO has a strategy in his head (however big it is) and if he knows his own limitations, these aspirations can become a key element in his company's success. Because it is motivation of this kind that has brought mankind to where it is today.

Your client's aspirations must be closely linked to the realization of his long-term vision and ambitions. These aspirations should never be daydreams; instead they must be based on the solid foundations of reality covered in the first three steps of this book. Your client needs to be able to relate his aspirations to a business road map. This road map need not be very detailed; often a company does not always know in advance how it will reach its goal and CEO's frequently have to make things up as they go along. However, it is vital that the direction in which the company is travelling is clear and understood.

Sometimes your client will be forced to take a step backwards in order to move forwards again (e.g. a cash flow crisis may necessitate the temporary laying-off of staff). This does not mean that they are going in the wrong direction; it simply means that they have to find a new way of moving forward, taking account of the economic and cultural circumstances in which they find themselves. Growth is very rarely linear. Mostly business grow via a sequence of expansion and contraction, with each phase of expansion being bigger than each phase of contraction or stabilization. You can compare it with the forward movement of an earth worm.

Before moving on to Step 5, check your client's mission statement and learn it off by heart. The mission statement should be embedded in the minds of all company staff and even, in some circumstances, in the consciousness of both suppliers and clients. Only move on to Step 5 when you feel that you have a full understanding of the company's real aspirations. If you move too soon, whatever steps you take next will lack focus and will be without true purpose. A five-star hotel on the wrong road is always worse than a two-star hotel on the right one.

You can call your intervention a success if, when you look back from Step 9 at the aspirations you identified in Step 4, you can say in all honesty that your solving of the problem has helped the client to take a step towards reaching these aspirations. However, if your problem-solving efforts have distracted your client from his real goals, then you must regard your intervention as a failure, even if you did solve the immediate problem. This may seem harsh - but it is nonetheless true.

Step 5

Decision time

DECIDING WHAT ISSUES SHOULD BE TACKLED FIRST
AND IS THE BUSINESS FULLY COMMITTED?

There are two key elements to Step 5. The first is deciding whether or not to try and solve the problem at all (is it too little too late and/or is the gain worth the effort?) The second, assuming you decide to go ahead, is deciding what aspect of the problem to tackle first.

Thus the decision-making emphasis at this stage is not on 'what are we going to do', but rather on 'are we going to do anything at all – and why?'. How committed is our client and how much energy should be spent? Exactly 'what' will be done and 'how' it will be done: these are matters which, in most circumstances, can be considered later.

Luckily, in most cases, taking a key decision or solving a complex problem does not come down to a single major issue. Once you start building the strategy to solve the problem, the decision-making process can be broken down into a series of logical steps, each of which can in turn be monitored against the desired results, with fine adjustments being made along the way to our desired solution. But first there is that key decision: whether the problem really should be solved at all.

Reasons for a 'let's go' decision:
1. You have a thorough understanding of the real issue at hand.
2. The urgency of the issue and the benefit of solving it far outweigh the pain of the effort.
3. Your client and their staff want the issue solved – they will be your motivators (without motivators, the chances of success are poor).
4. All involved have a genuine belief that the solving of the problem will make the future look more promising.

Reasons for postponing a decision:

1. A lack of understanding with regard to the true nature of the real issue.
2. Serious uncertainty or dissension with regard to the real benefits of the solution.
3. Belief in the value of solving the issue, but uncertainty about the ability to do so.
4. The urgency of the issue is secondary to other matters which need to be tackled first.
5. The decision to move ahead is dependent on factors outside your client's control (e.g. waiting on new finance).
6. More 'buy-in' is required from sponsors and other resources.

Reasons for deciding to abort:

1. The pain of solving the issue is disproportionate to the value of the expected result.
2. The problem is not affecting the business severely enough to warrant the risk of change.
3. You have insufficient 'believers' in any possible solution.
4. The problem is clearly too big for the resources available.

If you decide to go ahead (or indeed postpone), the next phase will be to develop detailed proposals that will give all the sponsors and the motivators a chance to re-evaluate the proposed solution, before giving the final go ahead.

FINDING THE DECISION-MAKER'S HIDDEN AGENDA

Even if you have made all the right arguments to support the taking of a positive decision, you may be disappointed with the outcome, if the decision-maker has a hidden agenda.

As in Step 4 (aspirations), we sometimes need to get to the bottom of the decision-maker's motivation. Just like the salesman in the lawn mower shop, we need to find the triggers that will turn a 'maybe' into a 'yes'; 'I am not so sure' into 'let's go for it!'

Often I see that the personal goals and ambitions of the CEO or the other directors are hidden behind the long-term vision of the business - and that these personal agendas are not necessarily shared with, or by, the rest of the management team. Private goals and ambitions must be taken into account by the interim manager, otherwise sensible solutions and suggestions could be rejected for no apparent reason. If, on the other hand, a solution can be found that takes the CEO a step nearer to his dream, there is a much greater likelihood of obtaining the conviction and the drive required to make the change a successful one. What people want and what they need can be two very different things. However, any solution that does not try, at least in part, to deliver what is wanted by the key players is almost bound to fail.

It is almost impossible to motivate people to stay away from the things they want. A doctor once told me that he had given up prescribing special diets or exercise regimes, because he knew his patients would never follow them, if it meant missing out on food they craved or changing a familiar routine, even though they knew that the diet or the exercise would radically improve their condition. It seems that even the threat of imminent death or disability is not enough to motivate some people in a new direction. But if we can incorporate personal dreams and goals into the solution, then the passion to inspire change can also become the fuel to bring that change about.

THE STORY OF THE STUDENT

I remember a time at school when one of my friends was listening to music instead of studying for the next day's examination. I asked him if he wasn't worried about failing his exam. 'Yes, I'm worried but not enough to study for it,' was his reply. If I had known then what I know now, I could have motivated him to action: I needed to encourage his desire to succeed and to do this I needed to tap into his dreams. In his case, it would have been enough to mention that the college to which I was applying had a ratio of 70% girls to 30% boys!

Implementing processes to ensure good decisions

The old saying which claims that there is no worse decision than no decision at all, is like many old sayings, this is very true. Even a bad decision s better than no decision. There is much to learn from the results of a bad decision, but ultimately nothing to gain. What we need is a good decision. But what is a good decision? Put simply, a good decision is a decision that you believe will not only deliver the required result but also – and more importantly - is a decision that you can sell to others. It is a decision that people will 'buy into', a decision which they can believe is the right one.

This 'sellability' is crucial. Some decision-makers might feel that they do not have to justify themselves (and sometimes this is true), but if the decision is going to require a high level of effort and 'buy in' from their colleagues, then being able to sell it is almost as important as the decision itself.

Some tricks and considerations when taking important decisions:

1. Have you completed and carefully reviewed each of the first four steps?
   a. Do you fully understand the true nature of the real issue?
   b. Do you understand its causes (the background which brought your client to his present position)?
   c. Do you have a good view of available resources: your client's 'cash, culture and competence'?
   d. Do you know the results you want to achieve? How will you know when you get there? Has your client defined his aspirations, mission statement and long-term goals?

2. Do you believe the objective is achievable? If so, why?

3. Can your client accept and support the decision to go ahead? Is your client likely to change his mind at the first sign of trouble? If you are in any doubt on this matter, you will need to ensure there is a structure in place to prevent backsliding at a later date, so that you keep to the chosen strategy.

4. Have you and your client openly shared your thoughts about the proposed solutions with others? Are these people knowledgeable, competent, mature and objective enough to give good feedback and advice?

5. Have you or your client documented the current situation and the proposed solutions?
   a. Ask others to read this documentation.
   b. Give them enough time to think it over fully (you know the details, but it will take them longer to get the full picture).
   c. Listen to their responses with an open mind; this is a time for careful thought.
   d. Spend more time discussing the responses with those with whom you least identify (even if they strike you as being ridiculous).

6. The person who is responsible for taking the final decision is the person who takes ownership of the proposed solution.

7. Do not be lazy. Never take on someone else's decision, just because you are still uncertain in your own mind or cannot be bothered to work it all through. If you do adopt someone else's solution, don't blame them if things start to go wrong. The dominant decision-maker must take into account the likely consequences of making an unpopular decision without first securing the support of those who will be affected by it.

THE STORY OF THE FAMILY HOLIDAY

This is typically something which happens on family holidays, when one of the part-ners asks: 'Shall we do X or Y?' They can't be bothered to work out the alternatives and are looking for the other partner to make the decision for them. But if you fall into this trap without sharing the thought process that led you to your decision, watch out! Later on you will be hard pressed to explain why you chose to climb 500 steps to the top of the temple in the midday sun! And you might also be confronted with: 'Whose idea was it to go on this ridiculous trip? I never wanted to come to Greece anyway – it was all your idea. I only did it to please you.'

---

8. In group decisions, do not rush through important votes. Keep discussing and debating until everyone agrees on the best way forward. It is not enough just to say 'trust me'; take the trouble to explain your reasoning and encourage others to do likewise. It is far better to have unanimous, albeit grudging, support than a discontented minority, who later will constantly complain, 'I told you so'. A lone dissenter in a group can lead to a disproportionate loss of support, energy and influence, because the whole group will have to waste time in justifying every step of the solution process.

9. Make simple flow diagrams or decision trees to chart the possible outcomes from different decisions. For example:

10. If time allows (and in 99% of cases it does), sleep on it - not just one night but at least two.

11. If you do not yet know what to do and if the business is not in any immediate danger, do nothing at all until you have decided upon a viable solution. This might seem to contradict the adage that 'any decision is better than no decision', but it does not. The reason is simple: most bad decisions are either born of laziness (not bothering to think the issue through) or (even worse) boredom. For example, if you are getting bored with your successful but routine business, you may decide to broaden its scope and expand into new areas which are less suitable.

Some of these points may seem exaggerated and in some cases I suppose they might be. However, they are all matters which need to be considered, particularly when we are dealing with issues that can have a significant impact on the profitability of the company (as opposed to routine improvements or minor changes).

Getting ideas accepted

Getting ideas accepted is nearly always a question of good timing and good knowledge of the company's hidden agendas.

Every teenager knows that if they want to ask their parents for something big, they need to prepare the ground first. In short, they need to do a bit of lobbying or, even better, get one of their siblings to do it. This means that when they finally ask the big question, at least it does not fall on entirely deaf ears. And it is precisely the same in business: preparation is everything.

A good idea raised at the wrong time and in the wrong place is most unlikely ever to get off the ground. In the mini-play on page 77, the characters illustrate how not to do it.

Figure 4 • An example of a typical decision tree

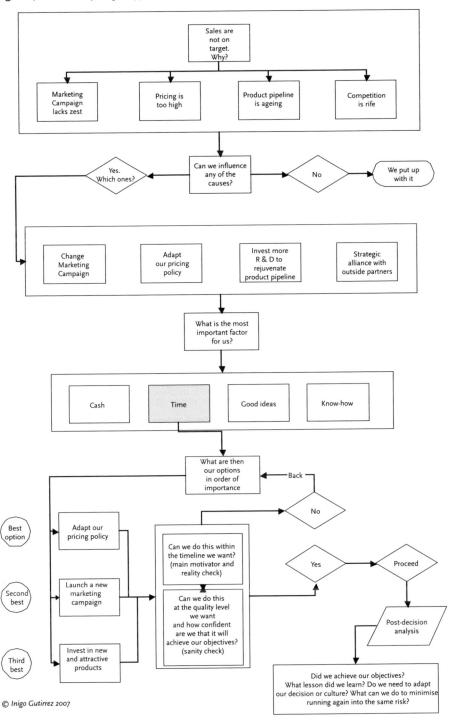

© *Inigo Gutirrez 2007*

Let's build a new showroom!

The scene is the weekly management meeting. Company X is an office furniture company and one of their problems is that they have too many meetings (too much time allocated, not enough structure).

Sales Director: Let's build a new showroom!
    Finance Director: Why? We only renovated our existing one the year before last?
    Sales Director: System G have a much bigger and nicer one than ours?
    CEO: How much business do they do in it?
    Sales Director: That's not the question. The question is how much would they do without it?'
    Marketing Director: For much less money we could build a virtual showroom that is never closed and allows our clients to explore our range in their own time. With modern technology we can even have remote salespeople join them in virtual space and guide them through the sales process, if required.
    Sales Director: We all know that's just fantasy. No one buys furniture without seeing it for real.
    Marketing Director: I wouldn't be so sure. If they know our name and they know what they want, our on-line technology could help them with all aspects of their design. It would be like the IKEA kitchen software but a hundred times better – I've seen it in a demo in Frankfurt.
    Finance Director: If, if, if.! I agree with the CEO on this one. I think that deals are done at our client's office and not in the showroom or on the website. If we make it that much nicer, we'll never get our sales force on the road. They hang around here drinking coffee far too much as it is. Our current showroom is fine! And besides, who is going to pay for it?
    Sales Director: When we close the Microsoft deal, we'll have plenty of cash.
    Finance Director: Plenty of cash to pay off our spiraling debts and to give the shareholders their long overdue dividend, more like!

Moral of the play
If the Sales Director and the Marketing Director had sat together beforehand and worked out a joint strategy, linking the new showroom to the wider concept of the

new virtual showroom; and if they had prepared all the projected revenue versus cost calculations for the financial director, including the NPV (net present value) of the investment; and if they had waited to raise the subject until shortly after the big Microsoft deal was concluded; perhaps then – and only then – could their 'dream' have been realized. Now it is completely dead. It will be almost impossible for them to raise this issue again, at least for several months. Human nature being what it is, the Sales Director and Marketing Director - who should be working together as a team to find creative ways of generating new business - are likely to continue splitting the company in its commercial approach towards its clients.

DECISION-MAKING MEETINGS

Before you begin, remember the Board Room Principle: if the building is on fire, the members of the board will meet very quickly and agree to immediately evacuate the building! If the decision is less critical, such as deciding the colour of the walls in the new staff restaurant, you may find that reaching a decision is much more difficult. All sorts of people will emerge to voice their opinion and you may unexpectedly find that the situation becomes very personal and heated!

Imagine trying to get a company to agree the look and feel of their new invoice. Even if the existing invoice does not comply with current financial rules and regulations, the task of trying to get the Finance, Legal, Sales, Marketing and Communications departments to all agree might prove to be so complex, that the company's managers may prefer to accept no solution and run the consequential risks of illegality, rather than taking a decision that does not get the full support of one department or another.

During the decision-making process, it is extremely likely that you will need to hold meetings to discuss particular issues, with the aim of taking a decision at the end of it.

There are a few ground rules that can help you achieve a good outcome.

1. Choose the participants carefully.
2. Do not, however, restrict your choice exclusively to people who you know will agree with your proposals. For example, do not time your meeting for the weeks when the financial director is away on holiday, so that you will be spared 'all that negative input'.
3. Make it clear to all the participants exactly what the situation is and why you have selected them for the decision-making meeting. This is a clever and easy way of building up a sense of team pride. It is also a way of reminding everyone of the specific skills for which you have selected them. Also ensure that everyone is properly introduced. A person commonly known for their software programming skills might on this occasion have been selected for some other specific talent, of which some members of the meeting might not be aware.
4. Let the participants know right from the very beginning precisely who is going to take the final decision.

    This is important. Are you going to take the decision by yourself or are you looking for consensus? Whatever you decide, you cannot change your mind, once you have announced it.

    The advantage of a consensus decision is that it is easier to win the support of the full team. Everyone contributes to making the decision and so everyone is more or less obliged to stick to it.

    A unilateral decision may be quicker and easier to obtain, but this will change the whole style of the meeting, making it a more formal, boardroom affair. In this case, the participants will be lobbying for their viewpoint rather than debating, a situation which can easily lead to a battle of wills rather than an attempt to seek the best way forward. The participants can also become lazy, if they feel that their voice will not be heard, because they have no blocking power. As a result, they might just keep quiet, with the excuse that no one asked their opinion. If it comes to a vote, the minority will feel that their views are ignored and will later spend a lot of energy in saying: 'I told you so', working to prove that the decision was not the right one. And indeed it is also possible that the majority might be wrong.
5. Let the meeting know when the final decision will be taken. Will the final decision be made at the end of the meeting or within the next 14 days? You need to give the participants a full briefing and a clear timeframe. This helps to focus the

discussions and will bring expectations in line with your strategy.

For serious issues that do not require an immediate decision, it is not a bad idea to set the meeting objective, such as 'coming to a consensus by the end of the meeting'. Force the meeting to make a decision - any decision that they can agree on - and then give them an additional 48 hours to mull it over. This focuses the mind on the decision and yet still leaves time for possible improvements.

I find it is easier to comment on a specific decision than to comment on a number of fluid possibilities. We humans are not as good at coming to rational conclusions as we sometimes like to think we are. Often pressure of time forces us to react quickly, yet at the same time we must also try to be objective. We must not fear that there is a tiger chasing us, when there is only the threat of one.

6. In decision-making meetings it is important to stay focussed on the subject and not to wander off in all directions.

7. It is important to keep a proper balance between 'serious' and 'lighter' elements, since anecdotes and minor diversions can sometimes help to keep things in perspective.

8. Make a few slides in advance, which clearly outline the essentials of the situation. This is not only useful for the other participants but will also assist your own preparation, since it helps you to focus on the real issues and on the core decisions which need to be taken.

9. As a rule of thumb, try and limit each meeting to one key decision.

Never propose more than three. Wherever possible, summarize the options for each decision by offering up to three alternative scenarios for the participants to debate and agree. These scenarios must be clearly summarized on your meeting slides (See 'Decision Summary' example page 82).

10. Select a good chairperson.

A good chairperson can conduct a meeting in precisely the same way as an orchestra conductor can create a brilliant performance, getting the most out of each and every player. They can ensure that a correct balance is maintained and that every voice is heard. They can bring people to the foreground and then return them to the background, once their message has been understood or is becoming repetitive.

11. In the event of sharply conflicting viewpoints, when people are simply not listening to one another, enforcing a consensus on a specific point can be a useful tactic. Make it clear that the meeting will not end until the participants formulate a proposition that everyone is at least prepared to support, even though they might

> **DECISION SUMMARY**
>
> *Option A:*
> Present the project business case as it is now and accept that if the new technology arrives during the next two months, then we switch to the desired solution.
>
> *Option B:*
> Delay the project & the business case approval process and wait fot the new technology to arrive (trading early cost savings for possible increased functionality and cost savings later on).
>
> *Option C:*
> Go ahead with existing technology, with as early as possible delivery deadlines, ignoring the new technology even if it comes in during the life time of the project (18 months).
>
> *Decision: go for Option: A, B or C?*

not all agree with it wholeheartedly. In these circumstances, people are obliged to listen, even to arguments they find difficult to accept.

12. In emotionally-charged meetings (most typically, meetings dealing with personnel matters or trade union/management conflicts) you need to employ strict rules. Sometimes I place an object in the middle of the table (preferably something not too hard or heavy) and hand it to the person who wants to speak. They can then speak for as long as they want and no one is allowed to interrupt them until they replace the object in the middle of the table. I then hand it to the next person who wants to speak. It is sometimes a good idea to call for a few minutes of silence after a speaker finishes, especially if what has been said was controversial or difficult. This again encourages people to reflect on what has been said, rather than responding with knee-jerk reactions.

13. Remember that human beings need oxygen. When meeting rooms are too small (which is often the case these days) or if the air-conditioning system cannot replenish the air fast enough, the efficiency of the meeting will diminish sharply, as the oxygen supply falls. It is good practice to open the windows (or doors, if the windows cannot be opened) at least every two hours (every hour in small

THE NINE-STEP APPROACH TO PROBLEM SOLVING

rooms). After two hours, call for a break, but instead of allowing everyone to just around the coffee machine, encourage them to step outside or even go for a walk. A short stroll is a good way to clear the brain and can have an amazing effect on unblocking an otherwise difficult meeting. A meeting should never run for more than two hours without a break.

14. Try not to call important meetings after lunch; in terms of performance, people tend to be at their lowest ebb after eating. Generally speaking, mornings are best for important meetings. If you want the meeting to last an hour or less, always set it for one hour before lunch – hunger is a good motivator for succinctness! Arranging last-minute meetings for late in the day is not a good idea. Some participants may become anxious because they need to dash off to collect the children; do not expect them to give you the same rational and intellectual arguments as they would if they were more relaxed (having made arrangements for the collection of children beforehand). I have witnessed too many bad decisions taken because people agreed to anything, just to get away from the meeting, in order meet important family commitments.

15. Good minutes make good meetings. Always write your minutes during the meeting and read them out loud after each significant point or decision. Ensure that everyone in the room agrees with the minute. Do not move on until an agreement on the minute has been obtained.

16. Circulate the minutes shortly after the meeting (within 24 hours).

17. Encourage participants to read the minutes and to react to them as required. This is important, otherwise your decisions will remain mere words on a page, only to be re-read later in the event of serious dispute.

18. A meeting without an agenda, fixed objectives and agreed minutes is nothing more than a discussion group and rarely produces anything fruitful in the long run.

A well-planned, well-structured meeting, working with a clear agenda and reaching clear decisions, is a highly efficient use of resources. Time wasted in meetings is one of the biggest avoidable sources of lost revenue for many companies.

Tip

Next time you are in an unproductive meeting, count up the number of people in the room, calculate their average cost per hour, double it to cover overheads and then add up the total. That is the real cost per hour of the meeting, excluding the emotional drain it has on everyone. The time has been wasted, money has been squandered and an opportunity has been missed which may never return. Don't forget to include the time that everyone spends after the meeting discussing how boring it was!

CONFERENCE CALLS

In today's world of immobility, caused by endless traffic jams and huge global distances, telephone conferencing can be an efficient and ecological way of sharing information and making decisions.

Conference call meetings need to be well structured. Punctuality is essential. Without the aid of body language, people are far less forgiving when others are late or do not follow the discussion closely. The chairperson should make a mental picture of all the participants and introduce them one by one, remembering to bring people in by asking them direct questions. It is vital to adhere strictly to both the agenda and the timing. Regular conference calls must never turn into afternoon chat lines. There should be no place for gossip or other irrelevant topics, although a bit of humour can help to break up tedious or difficult moments, as people wait for one of the other participants to come on line.

Repeating things which people say (to confirm that you understood them correctly), summarizing difficult issues and asking for feedback: these are all essential habits, if you wish your tele-conferencing to be efficient. Always have someone reliable to take the minutes and ensure they are circulated within 24 hours or, sooner, if the situation demands it.

Meetings with voluntary organizations

I have had some experience of chairing charitable meetings and it seems to me that they are much harder than commercial ones. It is difficult to insist on a course of action from someone who has no legal or contractual obligations. Volunteers cannot be instructed to do anything they do not want to do and they often have no commercial or management background. The whole operation is built on goodwill, loyalty and the mutual exchange of favours. If someone wants to leave an important meeting at a critical point, they can. You cannot sack or discipline them: you can only smile and say, 'Goodbye, see you next week'.

Afterthought

If we leave a thought overnight, why is it that we can often see things so much clearer in the morning? Psychologists say that this is simply because our emotional state has returned to a more normal equilibrium, allowing our thought processes to work better. If you compare the human brain to a standard computer, being in a state of high emotion effectively uses up all our 'processing power', enabling us to remain sufficiently calm to avoid 'doing something stupid', but not allowing us to do much more. Everyone knows that when the processor light on their PC is flashing intently, you simply cannot get the machine to carry out other processes with the same efficiency. Why should our brains be any different? The human brain can multitask - some people better than others - but not as well as we would like - and certainly not if it is using all its processing power to suppress our rising tide of emotions.

Step 6

STRUCTURING THE SOLUTION

BUILDING A SOLUTION PLAN AND CREATING THE PROJECT

The best way to escape from a problem is to solve it.
ALAN SAPORTA

In this section we take on board all the soul-searching covered in Steps 1-4 and act upon the decisions taken in Step 5. Here we create the structure for the new way forward.

Now that we fully understand the problem and believe that we have the ability and the will to solve it, the next step is organise to ourselves efficiently, in such a manner as to maximize our chances of success. Some (mostly large) companies create projects for almost everything that is not routine procedure; this is their way of being 'creative', while still controlling costs. In fact, companies with mature project structures, such as PMI or Prince 2, often require the project team to calculate the NPV (Net Present Value), based upon the profit which could have been earned if an equivalent amount of money had been invested in the stock market or some other financial system.

Any company that has been through the process of raising capital should understand the general concept of NPV, but in a project structure it helps more particularly to focus minds on exactly how much actual and 'virtual' cash will be spent. 'Virtual' cash refers to the cost of man-hours spent on the project by employees who would normally be doing something else. If you have employees that simply move from one project to another within your organization, their cost cannot be considered as 'virtual', because in theory your business should be able to survive without them. In any case, it is generally a good idea before starting any project to consider how much your business will improve as a result of the project, assuming you reach all of your project's KPIs (key performance indicators). KPIs are extremely important, because they are the tangible results of the actions taken within your project and are also the standard by which your project will be judged.

I am not too concerned about the type of project methodology used by a company, as long as everyone involved understands it. This means that it needs to be simple to follow and easy to apply. Many project structures are so complex and have such abstruse terminology that only trained specialists can master them. In these structures the project managers are highly specialized professionals in their own right. This may be good for large organizations with a number of concurrent projects, but for companies that want to solve a specific problem or implement a one-time change, it is preferable to adopt a more pragmatic approach, such as the one I outline below.

If you want people to contribute, they must understand exactly what is expected of them and to whom they are ultimately responsible. They also need to know the criteria by which they will be judged at the end of the project (where can they improve and where can their skills and talents be shared with others).

A well-defined project, with a strong communication plan, focuses attention both inside and outside the business. It announces that change is on the way and it provides both justification and a timeframe for the project. This helps everyone to put events into their proper context (what is going to happen and why).

The methodology framework proposed in this chapter has worked for me on many different projects, from turning around a small company with cash flow problems to the implementation of a global technology change programme.

Project managers in large companies, with numerous concurrent projects involving multiple departments, who are accustomed to a more formal and 'rigid' approach to project management, such as PMI, may be surprised at how effective this simple methodology can be. Newcomers to project management, on the other hand, may find that it seems top-heavy and cumbersome. However, I can guarantee you that the effort of putting the project framework in place will be more than re-paid by greatly improved levels efficiency in the course of the project.

GETTING IT DOWN ON PAPER: THE PROJECT CHARTER

The Project Charter (an example can be found in the 'download' section of the book's website) is the central document which presents in detail the various ideas, issues, tasks and teams involved in the project. It also includes the project objectives, goals, budgets, targets and timelines. It is not something that is set aside, once written. On the contrary, it is the daily road map which reminds everyone exactly what is going on, how, why, when and where. It is the 'bible' which will put everyone back on track in times of dispute (which are inevitable in any project). All project participants should read it from cover to cover. Every aspect of the Project Charter must be made freely available to all those involved: hiding any of its contents is to be avoided at all costs. People are not stupid: if the project is designed to downsize the business, it will not be long before this becomes obvious to everyone.

THE STORY OF THE TEAM MOTIVATOR

I once managed a large project, where a number of the team managers responsible for delivering key elements were likely to lose their jobs at the end. Some of them had more than 20 years of service for the company and the prospect of losing their work was a terrible blow. My challenge was to motivate them to deliver their input on time and within budget, when every nerve in their body was telling them to try and delay the inevitable for as long as possible. In such a situation the project manager has to make clear that there are just three options:

1. *They can get on with the project and commit themselves to deliver, with the aim of earning an excellent final project review from their employer, so they will have a better chance of being reassigned (or at least of having something impressive to add to their resume, should they be made redundant).*
2. *They can pretend to participate, but then play political games behind the project manager's back, possibly even trying to sabotage the project.*
3. *They can openly refuse to play along, thereby running the risk of being pensioned off early.*

In such cases, I always try to be frank right from the start – you need to obtain a level of commitment that goes far beyond usual limits. You need to show the managers that there is still hope, that there is still a way forward. Tell them that if they go through hell for you, you will do the same for them. But if you say it, you have to mean it. A manager who works extremely hard and efficiently on your behalf deserves to receive a personal recommendation from you that is much more than just a simple e-mail to his boss. You need to become his promoter within the company, seeking to

> *ensure that he gets transferred to another division at the end of the project. I have been assigned several 'hopeless cases' in my career, only to succeed in restoring their hope, their self belief and their basic tools for self development. Many of them came through the experience stronger and of more value to the company.*
>
> *Of course, there are always some employees who remain unresponsive and unwilling to change, no matter what you try to do for them. Don't waste your time with such people. If things are not working out after a few weeks, remove them from the project.*

THE PROJECT CHARTER INTRODUCTION

Before you begin a project, you should write a simple one-page document that clearly describes the nature of the problem, the opportunities to solve it, the reasons for the project's implementation and its importance to the business. This one page document, which will form the introduction to the Project Charter, should ideally be written (or at least signed) by the most senior person within the organization. In other words, by someone who people look up to and respect. If this is not the case with your CEO, it is imperative that the project should be 'sold' to its stakeholders by those within the organization who do command respect. Without the necessary commitment from top to bottom, the project will be harder to implement and the chances of solving the problem will be reduced. Even the best interim managers cannot guarantee results, if 'buy-in' is lacking.

No senior 'buy-in' = lack of importance = apathy and non commitment.

The introduction to the Charter should be written in simple language, using short and unambiguous sentences, in order to minimize the chance of misinterpretation. If you need to read any section more than once before the basic message becomes clear, keep on re-writing it until you get the balance right.

Elevator pitch

You should also write an 'elevator pitch'. An elevator pitch is a concise description of the project that can be given in the time it takes to ride an elevator, i.e. 30 to 60 seconds.

Elevator pitches are an essential tool for all managers, especially CEOs. I have met too many CEOs who were desperately searching for investment capital but who were incapable of explaining in a few words what their company does and why it is special. To be successful in business (as in life), it is essential to be able to communicate quickly and easily both what you do and why you do it.

Similarly, in project management you must be able to explain in brief terms what your project is about and why it needs to be carried out. This is essential if you are going to capture the mindset of others and attract the resources and commitment needed to get the project off the ground. You should learn the pitch by heart and be able to recite it in a natural voice (not too quickly), so it is not only understood but also believed.

The elevator pitch also needs to be in the hearts and minds of your personnel. If they know it and believe in it, the project will run much more smoothly later on. Never underestimate the networking capabilities of your employees; they are your ambassadors. Their ability to 'spread the word' is fundamental to the process of building commitment.

The 'boiler plate' is a shortened version of the elevator pitch and sums up, in a single sentence or slogan, the theme and purpose of the project and/or the company.

The objective and goals of the project

The next section of the Project Charter should contain the objective and goals of the project. For many people the difference between objectives and goals is not clear. This is not helped by the fact that many project managers and methodologies offer their own definitions. The important point to remember is that in your project everyone must think alike and must understand the same definitions.

The story of THE EUROPEAN CUP

I like to define the difference between objectives and goals by using a simple football analogy. The objective for a football team might vary from season to season. Last season the objective of the team was to stay in their division and not be relegated. For this season, it might be to qualify for the very lucrative European Cup competition.

In order to be certain of achieving their objective of playing in the European Cup, the team must end the football season as one of the top four teams in the League. They will only be able to do this if they win more games than the other clubs in their division. Consequently, the goal for the team is to win their game each Saturday. In other words, the winning of an individual game is not the objective but is simply the means by which they will reach their objective.

By the same token, if the team plays other matches that do not have any impact on their ability to qualify for the European Cup – national cup games, for example - the manager will not be too worried if the team wins or not - because winning will not take them any nearer to reaching their primary objective. Consequently, the manager might take the opportunity to rest some of his key players and bring in some younger ones for these 'non- objective oriented' games.

The story of THE COURIER SERVICE

My second example is an international parcel delivery company which was looking to increase the number of parcels delivered worldwide, whilst reducing costs at the same time.

Each department was given the opportunity to contribute. The IT department came up with a project title 'Deliver IT', which fitted neatly into the company's corporate message. In this case, the project's objective was to 'increase efficiency', an aim which it intended to reach by the setting of a number of goals. One of these goals was a collaboration with the HR department. Together they would introduce a 'follow the sun strategy' for client support and internal communications. The project would deliver a system whereby all employees could access the same information over the same system, thus allowing a 24-hour service to the client, by transferring support and logistical operations seamlessly from one time zone to another. A second goal was to reduce operational costs by replacing the old desktop IT equipment.

Company objective: To deliver more parcels at a reduced cost.

  Project objective: To increase efficiency in communication and client support – and thereby reduce costs.

'Deliver IT' project goals:

- *Replace all the aging (unreliable and expensive-to-run) desktop IT equipment with new state-of-the-art 'Thin Clients', allowing improved data sharing and complete flexibility within the business ('anyone can work anywhere any time').*
- *Re-image and/or replace all existing servers to link the Thin Clients.*
- *Reduce the number of software applications from 3,750 to less than 150.*
- *Introduce new working hour schedules.*
- *Establish a new global personnel training scheme.*
- *Create a 'one business, one team' ethic.*

KPI's were set up to evaluate the project's success. The KPI's included:

1. *Total cost reduction calculations set over five years. Efficiency was measured in terms of number of personnel required to handle X amount of support enquiries.*
2. *The cost of IT support (the fixed maintenance costs and the number of staff required to keep the IT systems up and running). The IT system and management teams were also given performance figures in the shape of an SLA (service level agreement) and uptime key performance indicators.*
3. *Client satisfaction levels, measured against a key set of verifiable criteria.*

Everyone in the project knew what their function was and how they would be assessed. The project was broken down into sub-projects and each sub-project had its own goals and KPI's. Each sub-project was given milestones to identify key stages by which progress could be measured against specific deadlines. Gates were established to identify the different stages of each project.

SUMMARY

In project management the objective is the manner in which we review the overall end result (the effect that we want to have) and the goals are the different successes that combine to achieve the objective.

CONFUSING MILESTONES AND GOALS

A milestone is a point in time when an important step in the project should be reached, such as the end of the design phase, the completion of a task or the delivery of a report or other specified object, product or service. A milestone serves as a marker or checkpoint on the project timeline, on the basis of which the project is judged to be on schedule or not. Milestones have nothing to link them directly with goals, whereas a goal is always linked to a result which is directly related to an objective. A milestone is always linked to a point in time, thereby marking the progress of the project.

THE STORY OF 'DELIVER IT'

For the project 'Deliver IT', a million dollars of ICT costs needed to be saved in the first year following its start up. An additional million dollars of savings was required as a minimum for each of the subsequent three years.

The key (major) milestones were:

1. *Approval of the project approach plan and business case: project start date + 40 working days.*
2. *Completion of the resources phase of the project: project start date + 50 working days.*
3. *Completion of the research phase of the project: project start date + 110 working days.*
4. *New desk top systems - roll out start date: project start date + 160 working days.*
5. *New desk top systems - roll out end date: project start date + 195 working days.*

Thus it can be seen that projects should be broken down into phases, with the milestones acting as checkpoints along the way. Some managers like to introduce 'gates' between each phase. Gates are procedural reviews whereby the project is briefly reassessed, in order to determine whether it has achieved everything envisaged within the phase in question and whether it should continue to the next phase. Normally this is a 'formality' but like all formalities it should only be continued if it has a real function and brings a real added value to the company.

Project methodologies, such as PMI and Prince 2, are very fond of gates and phases. Companies using these methodologies tend to have multiple projects running simultaneously, so that the phase and gate reviews are useful for senior management to keep track of developments (e.g. budget versus results, etc.).

However, there is a serious drawback with gate methodology. By introducing fixed phases and gates, the whole project has to work in a linear fashion. This can lead to problems, since the project goals are often forgotten early in the project and all focus switches to achieving the milestones. Simply working to obtain the necessary gate approvals, so that the project can move on, is not the objective of the project. If important issues are minimised by the project manager (in the hope that no one will notice and that the problems can be solved later on), serious consequences can result. This is too high a price to pay, simply for achieving a milestone. A second potentially serious shortcoming of this type of methodology is that not all phases can (in practice) be stopped or completed before a new one can begin. Life is not linear – and neither is business. For example, some companies adopt the following phase structure:

Figure 5 • A typical methodology for a technology implementation project

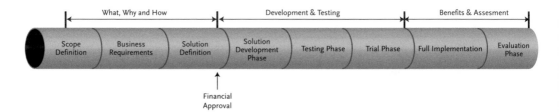

In phase three (solution definition) the solution strategy needs to be completed in time to receive financial approval. In theory this is fine: the project teams simply have to decide how they are going to deliver the project, which technologies they will use, etc., following which they will submit a business case and obtain approval for the project as a whole. After the business case is approved, the teams begin the solution development phase, where the detailed design needs to be completed before construction can begin. In practice, however, a key issue often arises at this juncture. All costs relating to work carried out before the financial approval phase are considered as 'Opex' (operational expenditure) and not as 'Capex' (capital expenditure). As a result, a great deal of pressure is placed on the project team to rush this stage through as quickly as possible, so that the Opex costs can be kept to a minimum (the reason being that Opex costs cannot be regarded as an investment and are therefore deducted directly from the annual profit & loss results, since they cannot be written off against income tax). This gives rise to two key issues:

1. Very often issues arise during the solution development phase which require more effort or more funds than was originally foreseen in the business case. This necessitates the use of a 'variance', a formal procedure whereby the project team asks for more cash and/or more time. The project manager could have played safe by asking for more funds during the original financial approval process, but this might have made the proposal look so unattractive that the review board would not have approved it. This is a common problem: the oversimplification of the project in the pre-business case phase, leading to more complex difficulties further down the line.
2. Under this system, development cannot begin until the entire design phase has been completed. If more rapid progress is required, you may find that your methodology is slowing down the process, rather than a lack of available resources. This is like the tail wagging the dog.

> *Tip*
> *An iterative methodology should only be adopted if the company has the maturity to deal with exceptions. If not, a 'free for all' breaks out, with the result that the methodology will be lost along with control.*

Imagine you are building a new office block. You may have agreed the type of materials for the main construction. You may also have agreed how many floors, offices, toilets etc. are required. But do you really need to know exactly what make of doors and windows you are going to use before you start laying the foundations? Matters such as the arrangement of the toilets and even the type of roof construction can often be decided much later, as long as the basic architectural framework is in place and is sufficiently robust to cater for minor alterations. Many buildings are well under way before the detail designs are completed. In the Hong Kong and Shanghai Bank (designed by Sir Norman Foster), the design for the director's seventh floor swimming pool had not even been considered by the time the main framework was going up.

Similarly, when I was the COO of a company supplying sophisticated software to the space industry, we were once told that it did not matter if our product was not 100% complete at the time of delivery, since it was going to be installed in a information-gathering system that was only to be activated once the space capsule neared its target. This target was a meteorite that would pass close to the earth in nine years time. So as long as we could upload our latest firmware from earth, we still had at least eight years of additional programming before the situation became critical. This is obviously an extreme case, but if our client had missed the launch deadline for the capsule because he was waiting for the final version of our software, his business would simply have collapsed, since the penalties for holding up multi-million dollar projects do not bear thinking about. This clearly demonstrates that often it is better to get your rocket into space rather than to spend too long on the ground deciding who is going to make the astronauts' seats, etc.

To recap: I am in favour of phases and gates, because they require both the company and the team to work in a structured manner. But I only like to use them if they can overlap, when necessary. A classic example is when you write your requirements and hand them to a supplier, only to discover that the supplier can deliver much more than you originally hoped for. He exceeds your requirements or may even change the way you approach a problem, purely because of his input to the solution. In other words, your requirements can be changed in the light of unforeseen solutions and technologies. If this were not the case, there would be little or no place for innovation. A good supplier drives his clients beyond their point of expectation, thereby delivering added value.

BUILDING A DETAILED PROJECT PLAN

In my opinion, there is only one tool readily available on the market which does the job simply and efficiently: Microsoft Project. This software programme can be used for a whole variety of applications, from defining the overall plan for large, complex business projects, right down to planning a wedding or family party. The beauty of the system is that it obliges you to follow a logical structure. There are many people who dislike Project but in my experience most of them have never really used it properly or have not bothered to learn its basics. The latest version guides you through the whole project process from start to finish and if you use a simple structure (like the one I suggest in this book) you really can hardly go wrong.

> **Tip**
> *Start off by typing every project-related action you can think of in the 'task name' column. In the beginning, I like to think of the main activities or 'teams'. Consider the following example: the organisation of a family party. First, you will need to identify the main activities: Speeches, Food, Wine, Music, Dancing, Location, Date, Invitation list, Budget, Finance, Transport, Accommodation, Create small committee, Contingency planning Next, you should try to arange these activities in a certain order or simply break them down further into logical teams of effort. 'Research', for example, would be a useful team group, allowing Location, Date and Accomodation all to be included in the same section.*

One of the most useful things about Microsoft Project is that when you have written down your tasks, you can apply timeframes and allocate people to each of them. During the project-building stage, you will think of many additional items (for the organisation of something as relatively simple as a family event there can be as many as 70 individual tasks), but these can be easily added and, if necessary, linked to other tasks which cannot begin until the new task is completed. By linking tasks, you can very quickly see what needs to be done, when and by whom. By reviewing the planning with others, nothing is left to chance and everyone feels that they have a role to play. In particular, they can see their dependency on others and the dependency of others on them. This is the beginning of the concept of a team.

THE NINE-STEP APPROACH TO PROBLEM SOLVING

THE CONCEPT OF A TEAM

It is commonly understood that a 'team' is a collection of people who work or play together, usually in close proximity. However, in today's modern world teams can be spread all around the globe. During one particular project, I managed a team of 78 people scattered over numerous different countries, many of whom I never actually met in person. For this reason, I define a team as being a group of people working together towards a common goal, no matter where they happen to be located.

As a famous motivational poster tells us, 'Trust is the emotional glue that binds a group of committed individuals into a team of people committed to each other'. I believe this to be true. If I do not feel that there is trust within my team, I will do whatever is necessary to *instil* it. In difficult times, a team with trust will pull together, whereas a team without trust will start to argue, focusing on each other rather than on the solution to the problem. But trust alone is not enough. You have to build a culture of respect, appreciation and even affection for one another, if you want to create a truly unified and passionate team. As far as I am concerned, passion is the one emotion which can make a difference between getting the job done and getting the job done well. I am not saying that the team members have to love one another (heaven forbid!), but they should at least have respect for each other's differences of opinion. If they can achieve this, in time they will move to a deeper level of mutual understanding and unified commitment.

> *Tip*
>
> *Microsoft Project is useful for helping to communicate the notion of a team, because it is a system you can easily 'share' with others. (Note: MS Project is not cheap, but the full version only needs to be used by professional project managers; others can read the project files with the Project Viewer program). A project manager can make best use of the system by simply printing out the charts and placing them on the wall. This two-dimensional representation helps to put items, timings and events into perspective.*
>
> *Some people prefer to use Excel for making project plans, but I have never found anyone capable of using spreadsheets in a way that others can easily follow. If you are likely to have to organise a number of projects, mastering MS Project, or a similar software programme, is the first step towards becoming a professional project manager.*

A project is often referred to as a 'programme' when it contains a number of separate elements, each with their own manager. If your project or programme involves different skill sets and teams, you do not necessarily need to plan in detail for all of them. As long as you have captured the key deliverables and milestones, you can leave the fine detail to the manager responsible for what I call the 'sub-project'. For example, using the family party scenario, the project manager does not need to plan how the food will be purchased and cooked. But if the food is going to be prepared by a caterer in the garden of somebody else's home, the project manager will have to create an MS task to check that the electrical supply is sufficient for the cookers, refrigeration and lighting, etc., as well as for any music and special effects which may be planned.

Once your project plan (or Gantt chart, as it is sometimes called) has been completed, you will need to have it carefully reviewed, not only by the 'client' but also by the key people responsible for the project's implementation. It is important that the review is not conducted line by line. This is too tedious and most clients will either simply answer 'Yes, that sounds fine' to everything you say, or else annoy you by questioning almost every task: 'Is that really necessary? I've never had any problems with electricity before.'

It is best to give the client a simplified overview. This is perfectly possible with Microsoft Project: as long as you have grouped the tasks together, you can simply collapse all the details and just show the highlights. If the client is being difficult by making needless alterations to timings etc, you can quickly expose all the sub-tasks to show them the complexity of all the various inter-dependencies. There is usually an audible gasp when they see all the effort and detail you have gone to.

> *Tip*
> *Always have an administrative assistant check that all the links between the tasks are in place. Then if you need to move the timeline later on, you can be sure that all the tasks will move together, saving you hours of work.*

Building a detailed project plan is time-consuming but fun, constantly prompting you to think up new and ever more varied dependencies. Always print your results and pin them on the wall – you will be surprised how many elementary faults you will find in them, especially when you show them to others. The purpose of this exercise is to do the impossible, to foresee the unforeseeable and to think of the thousand and one things that might go wrong – and then to pre-empt them, by building a formal structure which takes into account hidden issues over which we might have little or no control. In the example of the family party, the most obvious 'unknown' factor is the weather. Consequently, a contingency should be in place to make sure that the party will not be spoilt, if the weather is bad.

For most projects you will need a project organisation structure and chart. In the beginning, you do not need to add all the names, especially if you are not sure that the people you want will be available. At this stage, all you need to know are the skill sets required. I am often asked, 'What comes first: the project organisation chart or the Gantt chart?' The high-level Gantt chart must come first, because it is only when you go through the process of planning that you can assess what resources and personnel you really need. Many managers make the mistake of building projects around the people they know and have available: this inevitably results in some people being put into positions to which they are not well suited. For now, however, a general overview will suffice.

Involving the client or not?

It is generally a mistake to have the client involved in the project on a daily basis. The client can be the CEO or the board of directors, or even an outside company. In any event, you will need to agree with them in advance how they will be informed about progress, how frequently and exactly what input is required from them. It is not normally a good idea to invite the client to your regular progress meetings. Every project has its difficult moments, when the schedule looks seriously under threat or key suppliers unexpectedly pull out. At these moments you need to have a clear head - to think logically and to bang the table, if required. The last thing you want is a panicking client, running around like a headless chicken, undoing all your team's good work.

Emotional people tend to act irrationally. Remember that the client is emotionally involved with the project, whereas the project manager is only committed to the project - that makes a big difference. The project manager may at times show emotion, but he should never become emotionally involved. If he were a doctor, you would certainly not expect him to act irrationally in a medical emergency.

Figure 6 • A clear project organisation chart helps everyone to understand their overall responsibilities and the reporting procedures (both upwards and downwards)

Project – 'Deliver IT'

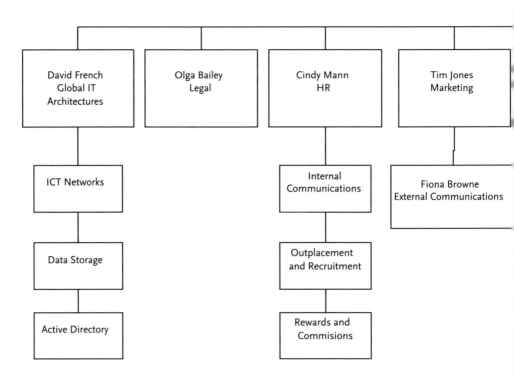

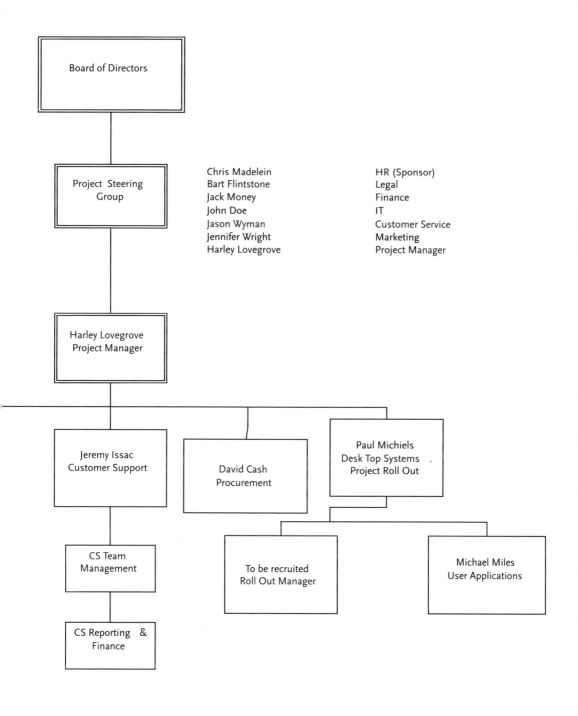

Board of Directors

Project Steering Group

Chris Madelein   HR (Sponsor)
Bart Flintstone   Legal
Jack Money   Finance
John Doe   IT
Jason Wyman   Customer Service
Jennifer Wright   Marketing
Harley Lovegrove   Project Manager

Harley Lovegrove
Project Manager

Jeremy Issac
Customer Support

David Cash
Procurement

Paul Michiels
Desk Top Systems
Project Roll Out

CS Team
Management

To be recruited
Roll Out Manager

Michael Miles
User Applications

CS Reporting &
Finance

Only when the project is running close to failure either on budget, scope, time or quality should the project manager raise the alarm with the client, but by then he should also have worked out a fallback scenario and how to implement it – preferably giving the client one or more options. In such situations, clients like to be given a choice: it gives them a feeling of control. However, they do not expect you to dump your 'unsolvable' problems on them.

When projects get really bogged down, it is sensible to swallow your pride and call in the assistance of trusted friends and professional colleagues for a second opinion. This is also one of the benefits offered by a project management group partnership, where like-minded professionals work together, each with their own particular skill sets and experience.

> *Tip*
> *Remember that a good, detailed planning (Gantt chart) can help to avoid 90% of problems, while a well thought-through risk analysis, coupled to a feasible fallback plan, should keep your project well and truly out of danger.*
> *You don't have to be like NASA (the North American Space Agency), with back-up plans for every imaginable scenario. NASA needs these plans because their technology is very much in its infancy: unproven, and extremely volatile Yet we can all learn a lot from NASA and any project manager who has not seen the film 'Apollo 13' or read the related book by Gene Kranz – 'Failure is not an Option' – is well advised to do so. Kranz's book is not just a spin-off supporting yet another Hollywood movie; it tells the story as it really happened. There is so much material and useful one-liners for a professional project manager to learn from (particularly in the middle of the story, when the crisis first arises) that it is well worth studying.*

Fallback plans and good project managers

Fallback plans and change control have nothing to do with the budget and everything to do with need. If your project is risky, you need to consider these matters very carefully. Failure to provide an additional budget and additional time for fallback strategies in a high-risk project is like playing with a loaded revolver - and that has nothing to do with professional management. On the other hand, a nit-picking manager, who always insists on examining all the risks, is most likely to be insecure – which means that he is probably a poor decision maker and therefore not a very good project manager. The best project managers are people who are creative, always finding a way out of a particular situation. They have excellent communication skills and can convince even the most stubborn person to follow in the required direction.

However, project managers can also be extremely dangerous; they can lead whole companies down the wrong path. Make sure that you check out their credentials first and always insist on seeing their detailed planning (just to make sure they have one!). Another good tactic is to ask the project manager's team members about the fallback scenarios for particular issues: if they haven't got a clue or have not been given a clear plan, these can be signs of a lazy or megalomaniacal project manager. In the worst case, it can mean both!

Obtaining the go-ahead

Your Project Charter is written; your plans are in place; your project organisation chart is completed. All you need now is the all-important go-ahead.

Depending on the size of the company and its methodology, a business case is usually required. This document can vary from a simple one-page summary, where costs versus benefits are briefly but clearly analysed, right through to a detailed study of some 100 pages or more, covering every conceivable aspect of the project. Some companies like to combine their business requirements with their business case. This is not such a good idea, because very soon these documents will need to be separated, with the business requirements going off to suppliers and other interested parties, while the confidential business case will remain within the company (possibly only being shown under a non-disclosure agreement to investors). Moreover, once the two documents become separated there is a strong risk of changes being made to the one but not to the other. It is therefore much better to keep them completely separated from the start.

Some people prefer to include the financial details from the business case in their Project Charter. This is acceptable but it tends to make the document too heavy and therefore seriously reduces the Charter's circulation potential. I prefer light project charters which can be openly distributed within the business, giving out a clear message of the need for change.

Further Reading

The advice and tips in this section are given on the assumption that the reader already has some project experience. If you are not familiar with project management or the writing of business cases and project charters, I highly recommend that you read one or more of the following books:

'One Too Many Projects' by Geoff Reis and Geoff Leigh; 'A Guide To Project Management Body Of Knowledge' from PMI; 'Organizing Projects For Success' by Vijay K. Verma; or 'Project Management' by Harold Kerzner.

In addition, on the Making-a-Difference website you can find examples of project charters, project plans and business cases to help you create your own project structure.

Step 7

RESOURCEFULNESS, RECRUITMENT AND COMMITMENT

ENSURING YOU HAVE THE RIGHT PEOPLE, RESOURCES AND COMMITMENT

In Step 3 we looked at the company's foundations; the assets and resources available to us. In Step 6 we structured the challenge which lays ahead. In Step 7, we will see how to get the most out of the assets and the human resources at our disposal and also how to recruit in the skills sets that we are still missing.

RESOURCEFULNESS OR 'HOW TO MAKE THE MOST OF WHAT WE HAVE'

In sport it is often said that an average team of committed players will always out-perform a team of better players who are too nonchalant on the pitch. However, the observation of any sports team playing over a single season will also demonstrate that the same resources, applied in more or less the same conditions, can often pro-duce widely differing results. There are no guarantees for success, either in sport or in business, but the creation of a winning environment is largely a question of belief and motivation. For this reason, it is the duty of every interim manager to get the most out of the resources at his disposal.

Apart from possessing the ability to motivate and to instil belief, an interim manager must also be very 'resourceful'. They need to be able to find solutions for every prob-lem thrown at them. They need to find ways of encouraging their team to believe that a solution is out there somewhere, just waiting to be discovered. They need to stimulate the team to think creatively and to take ownership of the problem, so that everyone becomes a part of the solution in one way or another.

If the mountain won't come to Mohammed, then Mohammed will have to go to the mountain. If the team cannot find a way to cross over the river, then they will have to tunnel under it. In other words, the interim manager needs to be able to inspire his team to think 'out of the box'. Resourceful people do this naturally.

Solving a problem with your client's own resources is far better for the morale and the culture of a business than going to the bank and attempting to buy your way out. It is commonly known that 'throwing cash' at a problem will seldom solve it - ask any investor who has repeatedly tried to keep a drowning company afloat by pumping in additional funds.

In some parts of Europe people refer to this combination of belief, motivation and resourcefulness as the 'Dunkirk Spirit' but I prefer to think of it as 'mankind triumphing over adversity'. To some, this phrase might sound a little bit glib, but when I watch the behaviour of successful CEO's and managers, I notice that they all have one simple thing in common: they are able to commit people into working for them. Be careful: they will use every trick in the book to coax you, too, and before you know it you might find yourself writing a report for them, even though you have not yet signed a contract! This is their standard tactic: they always look to inspire those around them to solve their problems. This makes their colleagues feel needed and motivates them to successful action.

> **Tip**
> *An interim manager who always tries to come up with the solution himself will end up with a lazy team that relies on him to solve all their problems. Solving problems requires concentration and concentration over a long period makes us tired. Human beings are naturally lazy, so if the leader says that he is going to solve the problem, his team will be happy just to hang around and let him get on with it. If his solution is a good solution, then they will come to him to solve all their problems in future. If his solution is a bad solution, they will very quickly lose faith in him as a leader. It is a no-win situation.*

I believe that we are all born with a great deal of resourcefulness, but that somewhere along the way this talent diminishes – at least, for many of us. The daily routine of life, combined with the natural tendency to avoid risk as our responsibilities increase, is enough to steer most of us away from meeting challenges head on. This can be demonstrated, for example, by the fact that children are better than their parents at playing computer games. Children are not pre-conditioned; they assume nothing and they will risk everything, even if there is only the remotest chance of success. However, by the time a person leaves full time education their risk curve is beginning to flatten out, as routine starts to set in.

If there are staff in your client's company, no matter how junior, who you judge to be resourceful, make sure that you include them one way or another in your project. I have known office cleaners with more insight and common sense than many *cum laude* graduates.

In short, your client's human resources are the key to your success. Getting the most out of them and sustaining their belief that they are following a winner is all that really matters. This applies equally to the people you work with beyond the walls of the company: bankers, investors, suppliers, shareholders, family and friends.

If the suppliers also believe that your client is a winner, you will be able to get better prices, longer credit lines and faster deliveries. However, if they think that your client is a potential loser, the results can be catastrophic: they will withdraw their credit, increase their prices, cover their risks and give priority to your client's competitors. Questions of confidence have brought many stable companies to their knees. The winning ethic is a fundamental part of a company's culture; its ability to overcome adversity is often the difference between recovery and collapse.

RESOURCEFULNESS WITH CASH AND CLEAR THINKING

When you need to work out how you can save on costs, never forget to involve the 'less important' people in the company. Secretaries who can stretch the petty cash balance beyond its usual limits often have far more practical financial know-how than many qualified accounts managers. Never let anyone tell you not to be mindful of small amounts, because 'it makes no difference'.

I once worked for an organisation that was sinking rapidly. One day the financial director said to me, 'What's the point of stopping the free soft drinks now? That will only buy us a few more hours over the next six months.' In one sense, of course, he was right, but in another sense he was also completely wrong. As long as you continue to give free beverages to well-paid personnel, they are never going to take cost-cutting seriously. Stop the free drinks, turn down the heating two degrees and ask them to help the reduced cleaning staff by emptying their own waste bins: they will soon get the message. They will begin to think differently and will understand that for now all efforts, however small, must be focussed on saving the business. Conversely, the same is often true if the company is successful. If new investors obtain a majority of the shares everything will change. The endless free drinks will stop, to be replaced by a Coke machine vending at a price. The new investors will not want to see wastage.

If a business is serious about reducing costs, the entire company mind-set needs to change – directors included. The cost savings may be announced as being temporary, but they need to be announced. Personnel should be encouraged to make suggestions and contributions. It always amazes me that the bigger the company, the fewer the free 'luxuries' available to staff and visitors. I have rarely seen large corporations in competitive markets offering free Coke or giving out expensive laptops in a carefree manner. On the contrary, it is often the big companies that insist on laptop sharing and the reduction of office floor space per person, in order to fit in as many people as possible.

I once worked with a small to medium-sized software manufacturer, who said they were going to have to move to new premises because they were running out of space. I showed them some photos of corporate open plan offices and said that if Shell can work like this, why can't you? They had enough wasted internal space to house 40 % more staff, whereas they only needed to recruit another 10%. Of course, it is pleasant for staff to work in a spacious environment, but it is better to work in cramped conditions and be competitive than to stay at home hunting for a new job, because the CEO has wasted hard-earned investment money on a smart new office.

The following brilliant example of resourcefulness comes from an architectural practice in Warwickshire, England.

THE STORY OF THE ARCHITECTS PRACTICE

The architects practice was expanding rapidly and had more work then they could comfortably handle. They had placed employees almost everywhere in their building: one was even working under the stairs! Being creative, they made the spaces attractive and there was a genuinely good feeling about the place. Nevertheless, in time the space eventually ran out and the practice still desperately needed to hire more architects. The problem was how to attract them to a small historic town more than 100 miles from London? One day, one of the office juniors paid a work visit to the ar-

---

chitects' department in the local town hall. 'My goodness,' he said to the clerk. 'You certainly have a lot of space here'

On returning to his own office, he bumped into one of the senior partners and joked, 'I've solved both your staffing problem and your accommodation problem in one go. All you have to do is buy the local authority's architectural department; they've got loads of space, people and work!' This was during 1990's, in Margaret Thatcher's Britain, when privatisation of public services was all the rage. And so it was that a few months later, Warwick Council became the first local authority in Britain to sell its architecture department. In the building recession that soon followed, it was this department that helped to keep the practice afloat during a period of dramatic downsizing, since there is always a need for the restoration of public buildings and for the construction of new schools, fire stations, bus shelters and day nurseries.

Being resourceful is about looking around you and thinking creatively; looking for other people or companies who can take on the work that you are currently doing; farming out, farming in, breaking moulds, putting two and two together to make five – whatever works. Some people are often at their most resourceful when under stress; these are the people you need to talk with, when handling difficult situations.

The term 'resources' includes much more than people, hardware and cash. Resources can also include public opinion, market perception, goodwill and public awareness. If you can attract awareness and obtain public support, this can only help to give you and your staff the feeling that everything is possible. Public awareness of an exciting new project within an organisation can also help you to attract the right people internally. You will soon have them knocking on your door or inviting you for lunch, asking, 'What's this I hear about a new project?'

Never underestimate the networking capabilities of your project team and your client's employees; they must be and will be your ambassadors. An honest and fair human resources policy, coupled with a culture of hard work, achievement and fun, is the best environment you can create to encourage the best people to come and work for you at a realistic price.

RECRUITING PEOPLE

The ability to attract the best people to their team is an important skill required of all interim managers.

This is a skill which we begin to learn on the school playground. Two pupils elect themselves as captains and they take turns to choose their team from the crowd of eager children standing in front of them. The winning captains know that they need to choose the best players, not their best friends. This is a wise policy, because they know instinctively that when their team wins, everyone on the team will become their friend. The weak captain chooses the players he likes best, hoping to rely on their loyalty. But the strong captain knows that loyalty is only a matter of offering more than the other captain - and in any kind of game (no matter what anyone says), losing is never as much fun as winning. Winners hug one another, even if they hate each other; losers blame one another, even if they love each other.

When recruiting 'new faces' for his team, an interim manager should never simply consider old friends, well-liked colleagues and other 'convenient' people. The tougher the challenge, the more discerning he must be. A basic rule is to avoid nostalgia: the past is over and time often does curious things to people.

A common mistake is to forget that it is now more than five, ten or fifteen years since you last worked together with someone. Since then, the enthusiastic young subordinate you once knew has grown up, started a family, put on a little weight, achieved a significant increase in salary and is generally not as energetic as he used to be. So start with a clean sheet and see who else might be available. A golden rule is only to employ people who are peaking or who are at least on the way up.

Most people want to work for a winning team. Winning teams can afford to pay less for their top performers, because the players want to be in the spotlight. It is frequently the second or third best company (or football team) that has to offer massive wage packets to attract the right people. In football, every player wants to play in the European Champions League. If the club the player is about to join has just missed qualification, it could be a year or two before the player is able to achieve his goal. This means that however high the salary on offer, the club will always be his second choice.

If you want to hire the best, you need to define the kind of people you are looking for and then cultivate the environment to which they are most likely to be attracted. The ability of your client's employees to spread the word and to raise the level of expectation is a fundamental element in this process. When a company has to follow the traditional route of using advertisements and agencies to recruit an outsider, it takes much longer and costs much more than when an employee says to a friend, 'I'll see if I can get you in'.

Function Descriptions

Before you contemplate recruiting anyone (even internal personnel), write out a function description for each position that you need to fill (an example of a function description and a blank template can be found on the www.making-a-difference.be website, in the 'download' section). This is not an optional requirement: I don't care how good a person is, or who wants them, I need to see a function description before I agree to move forward with a recruitment of any kind. Failure to do this is merely postponing the inevitable (i.e., wasting your time), since you will eventually need a description if you are to brief your HR team or use an external agency. Besides, how can you know what you are looking for, if you have not written it down on paper?

- What is the function?
- What is their role?
- How will they be assessed?
- What qualifications/skill sets do you expect?
- What are their specific tasks, in order of importance?
- Who will they report to?
- What authority will they have?
- What personal characteristics are you looking for; good communicator, team player, assertive, pro-active?
- How long is the contract?
- Where is the person to be located?
- What working hours do you expect?
- References requirements; ex-bosses, colleagues, tutors, friends, etc.

All these questions are basic and many of them will be common to most projects. A typical requirement for an international project might be: 'prepared to travel at short notice' or 'must work flexible hours, to take account of communication requirements with project colleagues in China and the US'.

Making a function description saves a lot of time for everyone, especially the candidate. For this reason, it is a wise move to ask the candidate at the beginning of an interview 'Have you read the function description?' If the answer is 'yes', follow up immediately with the question: 'Just for the sake of clarity, could you please describe to us, in your own words, the function that you are applying for.'

You will be amazed how some people 're-interpret' even the most rigid of function descriptions. You may quickly establish that the person has either not read the document or else has a completely false image of the position he is applying for. In cases of this kind, you should hand them a copy of the function description and ask them to read it again, carefully. When they have finished, ask them the following three things:

1. 'Having read the function description, does the job still interest you?'
2. If yes, why?
3. Add: 'From now on, we would like you to answer any question we ask on the basis of your personal experience and with regard to the job description you have just read.'

To carry out a good interview, you need to go into depth. For this reason you should allow about an hour per person, including 10-15 minutes for writing and comparing notes afterwards. If the candidate is obviously not suitable for the position, check your pre- recruitment procedures and work out how they managed to slip through the net.

Interviewing

Whenever possible, I like to interview people with a colleague. I prefer to select a trusted member of my team, who is likely to have a different point of view from my own.

I like to work with a matrix interview form, which I use to remind me of the important questions which need to be asked. I also use this form to write my notes on. An example of a matrix interview form and a blank template can be found on the www. making-a-difference.be website, in the 'download' section. The use of the question matrix should be discreet. If the candidate is saying something which could be considered confidential or personal, stop writing and put your pen down, so that he feels more secure. In this way, you will be able to draw out far more information (assuming it is relevant).

In addition to an interview matrix form, I also like to work with a simple candidate assessment sheet (also available on the website), customized for each vacancy. This is essential if you have a number of candidates for one position. The idea is to identify a number of key skills or salient points which the ideal candidate must possess. At the end of each interview, give a score out of ten for each key point and add up the total. The assessment sheet will help you to focus your thoughts and impressions, allowing you to come to a balanced decision. After you have completed the sheet, it is a good idea to discuss your findings with your colleague, exploring areas of disagreement, in order to see if something serious has been overlooked. If necessary, you should recall the candidate to discuss any particular points of confusion. Whatever else you do, never fill in the gaps by guessing.

If you are interviewing many people for a number of different positions, it is easy to forget which candidate is which. When interviewing people, I like to have their CV in front of me and I generally insist on a photograph of the candidate.

I knew a manager who once hired the wrong person because he mixed up the notes and names of two different candidates. Apart from the embarrassment, much valuable time and money was wasted on all sides before this avoidable error was put right.

Interview techniques (observe, question and listen)

Always take time to look at the candidate's shoes; shoes can say a lot about a person. Notice their fingernails and hair. Does the candidate look you in the eye or keep glancing away? Are they nervous in the beginning? How long does it take them to settle down? After ten minutes or so, give the candidate a few 'hints' that the interview is going well; this will help them to relax - and will also put them off their guard! A few carefully chosen questions at this point will 'trick' many people into telling the truth, especially if you follow up your questions with a well-placed 'why'. For example, 'Do you consider yourself to be a good people manager?' 'Why?' You could then follow with a third question: 'But why do you want all the bother of having to discipline people for arriving late or for not completing their work on time?'

If you are not convinced by the candidate's answer, ask for more information or change the subject and come back to it later – but in a different way. For example, if you do not get a satisfactory answer to the question 'Do you consider yourself to be a good people manager?', you can try again later with 'Do you think of yourself more as a team player or as a manager?' Or perhaps 'How big was the biggest team you have ever managed?' Always ensure that each question you ask is qualified by another question. For example, if the question was 'How big was the biggest team you have ever managed?' follow up the candidate's answer by asking them the name of the company they worked for. You can then take the questioning to a deeper level, with probing queries such as: 'How many of your staff gave you problems? What kind? How did you deal with them?' Ask for examples.

During interviews, people can often behave like vending machines. In the beginning, they churn out stock answers to stock questions, saying whatever they think the interviewer wants to hear. However, with a little bit of skill, a good interviewer will soon find the right questions to ask, in order to obtain the required information. It is the interviewer's fundamental role to move beyond superficial appearances and to build up a real picture of the person in front of him. More importantly, he must assess what impact the interviewee is likely to have on the team.

Always be polite and respectful during an interview: after all, you are dealing with people's emotions. If you push the right buttons, some candidates will open up and often say quite personal things, which you must keep confidential.

Remember also that some interviewees may be spies, planted by a competitor to find out more about the company. This is more likely if the position has been advertised in a paper or on the internet. You would be surprised how many 'amateur' interviewers give away valuable commerical information about their business during an interview, especially to applicants for sales or financial positions. Remember that whatever you tell the candidate, he will probably tell someone else. In this respect, your conduct during the interview will not only reflect on yourself but also on your client's business.

Take control during the interview. The candidate needs to find out about your company and the job, but this can easily be accomplished through the combined use of the job description and the company website. Your task is to arrive at a professional opinion on the candidate after just half an hour's conversation – and you can only do this if you work in a structured fashion. For this reason, interviews are best conducted by two people ('good cop, bad cop', one friendly and reassuring, the other direct and tough).

Always ask for references, not only from people for whom the candidate has worked, but also from ex-colleagues who have worked for the candidate. If you like the candidate and you think that you might want to recruit him at short notice, do not forget to phone the references before you take him on. Most mistakes are made with the appointment of instantly likeable candidates, since their very 'likeability' means that their interview was probably lacking in objectivity.

Recruitment for projects is different from recruiting for permanent positions. The whole process generally needs to go much faster and you cannot afford to make mistakes – you simply do not have the time.

If you are not a good interviewer, find someone who is. Prepare your questions beforehand and have key members of the team assess the candidates. Ensure that they also prepare their questions beforehand and review them before the interview takes place. Give them guidelines with regard to the information you require.

> **Tip**
> *I like to ask experienced secretaries or female project members to meet recruits at reception and bring them to the interview room. It is my experience that most women are better at reading people than most men – they have more of the intuitive powers that men tend to suppress. In most companies with more than 10 female employees, you are likely to find at least one who has strong skills in reading people. Your receptionist should also be consulted. They are the first person to see the candidates arrive, they greet them and perhaps offer them coffee. They see how restless they are while waiting. They know within a few moments whether they 'like' them or not.*

In the final analysis, successful problem-solving or successful project management is not really about the team, the manager or how much cash you have at your disposal; it is a question of the amount of commitment you have.

But what is 'commitment'? This simple, three-syllable word is easily spoken but too often carries little or no meaning. 'I'm committed to the project, it's just that I need to leave on Wednesday and Friday at four o'clock because I have my dance classes'; 'I am committed to the project, but I simply don't believe that it will succeed'; 'I am committed to the project, it's just that I have lots of other things to do that are more important right now'. These are plain abuses of the meaning of the word 'commitment'. Of course, there is no direct link between levels of commitment and the working of fixed hours. However, if your team is truly committed, they will ensure that the project is delivered on time, even if it means giving up every other dance class in order to attend important evening conferences.

THE STORY OF THE AMERICAN LAWYER

An American lawyer once gave me his definition of commitment. 'You're a Brit, Harley,' he said. 'So tell me, what are the two most important ingredients for an English breakfast?' 'Eggs and bacon,' I replied. 'There you go,' he said. 'That's the difference between involvement and commitment.' 'How so?' I asked. 'Well,' said the lawyer, 'in order to prepare an English breakfast you need two animals: a chicken and a pig. The chicken is involved in the meal, but the pig is committed.'

I am not, of course, suggesting that your team should lay down their lives for you and work themselves into an early grave. Nevertheless, they must be prepared to give you and their fellow team members their highest level of commitment.

Unfortunately, commitment from your team alone is not enough; commitment needs to be 'end to end' throughout the company - from the directors and any other key stakeholders, right down to your team members and those with whom they will interact. Sadly, in many cases this is wishful thinking. As a first essential, get your project sponsors and your team committed (and keep them that way). Later, you will need to prepare the ground to obtain commitment from the employees affected by the project.

If you are trying to build commitment, but you find yourself surrounded by whiners, it is important to do something about it quickly.

My father could not be described as extremely sociable. He was a good man, a fine architect and (for the right kind of employee) a caring boss, but he had no patience with whiners, who complain and moan. As a child, when I grumbled about this or that, or was being generally miserable, he would say: 'Cheer up or clear off!' Not the kindest words a father might say to his son, perhaps, but they at least had the virtue of being frank and honest. I have used the phrase myself on more than one occasion, quite effectively in certain situations. If you want to get on with a task, the last thing you need is to be dragged down by whiners, especially if they are whinging about things that are not directly related to the task in hand, such as their boss, their last pay rise or their working hours. Dissatisfaction and unhappiness are contagious and you will soon have a number of people saying: 'How come I don't have the kind of company car he has?'

> **Tip**
> *My advice is to take the whiner aside, listen to their problems and give them some home-work to do. Ask them to make a list, preferably over a weekend, of what is most important in their life; also what they most enjoy and what they most dislike about their work. Spend an hour with them, in order to try and understand their needs and what motivates them. You might find a quick solution and earn their respect for it. On the other hand, if they remain negative, especially towards others, you should tell them bluntly that they need to get their act together - otherwise they won't find a place on your team.*

Every team member is worth at least an hour or two of your personal coaching time. However, if they fail to respond, do not hesitate to remove them from the project. This is not often necessary and you will be surprised how successful this technique can be. Most people manage to work out their priorities and decide to commit themselves. Those who do not are at least able to decide what they want and usually leave of their own free will. Others may accept the assignment while they wait for the right opportunity elsewhere. As long as they work well and provide good value for money, it is of no importance if a position in your team is not their ultimate life-long ambition. In this respect, it is essential to keep a balanced view: you must understand that your client's business is not the centre of the universe for everyone.

There are two main kinds of commitment: internal and external.

Internal commitment comes from the team members themselves. It is the belief that they can carry out the tasks assigned to them within the given time frame. It is the measure of how motivated they are and also an indicator of the extent to which their personal goals are being met by their project goals (align these and you are onto a winner).

Internal 'buy-in' also gives the team its homogeneity. How tightly are they bound together? How much trust is there? These non-physical resources (as they are known) are of crucial importance. If you invest time in your team (both as a group and as individuals), your effective resources may increase ten fold. It is an exponential curve that expresses the difference between a motivated and integrated team and a group of individuals without commitment or trust.

Commitment from outside the team is almost as important as commitment from within. A well-oiled, motivated team that is constantly running up against external opposition will quickly become despondent - and therefore less effective. If you do not secure external 'buy-in', it is probable that the people you need as allies will turn against you at the first sign of a trouble. Some may be actively hostile, while others may confine themselves to negative comments, such as 'I never thought this project would work'.

The key targets for external 'buy-in' are:
1. All people who will benefit from the project
2. All those who you might need in some capacity or other
3. All doubters
4. The company's dominant coalition
5. Middle management
6. Those excluded from the team
7. Those negatively affected by the result of the project
8. Shareholders, project sponsors and/or financiers
9. Clients, distributors and suppliers (as appropriate)
10. Journalists and press agencies (as appropriate)

THE NINE-STEP APPROACH TO PROBLEM SOLVING

For each target you might need to build a separate channel strategy. Ignore them at your peril! If you do not have good personal contact with a particular target group, put your ego aside and choose the best person for the job. You will be surprised how effective the most unlikely people can sometimes be.

THE STORY OF THE SCEPTIC AND THE SECRETARY

I once promoted a secretary to a fairly senior position in a project team. She was obviously grateful to be given the chance and promised that she would do everything she could to prove that I had made the right decision. One of my biggest sceptics (and a potential block to the project) was a male colleague who was fond of her but disliked me. She spoke to the sceptic about the project, about how important her role was and how she had created a structure which she thought would work. The sceptic was not convinced: 'With your boss, you'll never get anywhere. He'll take all the credit for himself.' 'Don't worry about that,' she replied. 'I've learned from you. He's not a problem for me, as long as I can keep my part of the project on track.' With this, the sceptic pledged his allegiance to her and a serious potential obstacle was removed. In future, I routed all communication to his department through her.

As long as your methods are legal, well-intentioned and not dishonest or immoral, any and all means should be used to win external 'buy-in'.

REMOVING BLOCKERS

Another crucial talent required by a successful interim manger is the ability to cope with resistance and to deal with 'blockers'.

A true-life example of how to handle blockers:

THE STORY OF HAROLD

I will never forget two colleagues who worked for me on an international project which I was managing. I was based in Brussels and they were based in Washington DC (USA). One of them was an employee with more than 25 years of service and I was an interim project manager with seven weeks experience in the company. Harold (one of the colleagues in question) was assigned to me as 'an experienced manager with a strong background in IT'. He worked in the US head office and had been responsible for ICT purchasing and the general management of the desk top systems. Harold reported directly to the ICT Director US, a man with years of experience in the company, who drove an expensive company car, always wore sharp suits and liked to look 'important'. He was the key man in the US, close to the Global Finance Director and personal friends with nearly everyone who could help him to maintain his dominant position.

As we sat around the boardroom table with my 13 other managers for the launch of the project, these two were by far the most positive and most forward-thinking. They received the Global IT Director's introductory speech with warm applause and vigorous nods of approval. I could easily have been fooled into thinking that they were going to be my strongest allies. However, experience had already taught me that work situations in which the head office was European and the operational staff were American could be fraught with difficulties. What looked bright and shiny on the outside could often be quite a different colour underneath. Most American professionals are used to working in an environment where their own companies or departments are the leaders in their market sectors. They dislike it intensely when a European company (especially from a small country with a population no bigger than a major American city) tries to advise a US division on best practice.

The difficulty for the project was that I needed 'buy-in' from these two men, since the project would radically change the way in which my clients' employees would work in the future. In fact, many of the IT staff involved in the project were likely to lose their jobs at the end of it. Within a week of meeting them, it became clear to me that both these men were potential candidates for redundancy, especially Harold's boss. His position had already become obsolete - he was too expensive and offered no real value to the business. All ICT decisions were now being made in Brussels. On the other hand, Harold was an experienced manager who might be able to adapt to a new position within the business. What I needed to do was to ensure that the tasks I set Harold could be monitored accurately at a distance, so that I was always in a position to assess the current state of play.

I told Harold that if he worked hard on the project, I would recommend him for a new position. Even if no new position was available, his exposure to new technologies would make it easier for him to find another job. There were rumours throughout the project team which suggested that I should not expect too much from Harold and certainly nothing from his boss. Despite my best motivational techniques, I could clearly see from the content of his weekly reports that all drive and ambition was lacking. The reports arrived on time, but he was not able to follow the timelines set for the project.

A few well-targeted phone calls uncovered a couple of interesting points. Although Harold seemed to be committed to the project, he was simply unable to follow it through: he needed his hand held every step of the way. To make matters worse, his US boss kept giving him advice which deliberately complicated even the simplest issues. In all the years that Harold had worked for the company, he had never been so closely managed (he reportedly said to a colleague that 'the new project manager is riding me like a bike!').

In the end, I reported back to my client that, as far as I was concerned, Harold's added value to me was almost zero. In fact, he was more of a hindrance than a help. Moreover, his boss was almost certainly blocking the project to such an extent that you could reasonably describe his actions as sabotage. To your face and in correspondence he was always polite, helpful and friendly: 'I would love to help you but....' Behind your back, however, he was inventing all possible reasons to block the project and make it fail, in the hope of securing his position in the US and re-building his power base. Within three months, he was removed from the company and Harold was told that at the end of the project he would be replaced. This left me in the uncomfortable position of having to find work for someone who was only interested in stretching out the project as long as possible. As a result, Harold was also removed and placed on 'gardening leave'. If people cannot be of help and you cannot sack them, send them home and keep them there until someone else comes up with a better idea.

> *In the corridor across the hall from Harold sat another of his American colleagues, who worked for the same obstructive boss. Unlike Harold, this man tried hard and understood that being supportive was the best means of ensuring long-term employment security (a not unimportant consideration in the US, when you are over 45 years old, like Harold was). He was also aware that there might not be any work for him at the end of the project, but he realized that compliance and commitment were his only chance. He gambled well, often going against the wishes of his US boss and colleagues. Result: after the project he was promoted to a position that suited him well and gave him the reward he had gambled on.*

Tip

The golden rule, at least in the beginning, is to take everyone at face value. Do not show any signs of doubt; instead, be positive and listen. On the other hand, you also need to remain a little mysterious; don't give your staff the feeling that you will be a pushover. Be precise in what you say, give the impression that you are extremely disciplined and expect everything to be delivered early, or at the very least on time.

Motivating people who think that they are about to be made redundant is not an easy task. You have to learn to cope with their mood swings. One day they will be enthusiastic, believing that everything will work out. The next day they will feel that everything is futile and hopeless. If they put their faith in you and you show any signs of insecurity, or if they are confronted with what they regard as an 'insurmountable problem', they will be completely lost. This is not pleasant, but it is nonetheless the reality of the situation in which you find yourself.

If you act on behalf of a business which has serious cash flow problems, so that downsizing is a very real likelihood, almost all your employees will have mood swings to a greater or lesser degree (only the inexcusably arrogant or foolish will believe that they are irreplaceable). The best advice I can give is to impose strict discipline. If the weekly reports are submitted on Monday morning, set a fixed time, such as 1000 a.m. At 1005 a.m. start chasing up anyone who is late and tell them that next time they will not be chased. Let them understand that this is not acceptable behaviour from a professional manager. Impose yourself as a friendly but strict manager, who is not prepared to let his project fail because of the sloppiness of anyone in his team.

THE NINE-STEP APPROACH TO PROBLEM SOLVING

There is a world of difference between imposing discipline and patronising your staff. You do not need to be a sergeant major and shout instructions, but you do have to be firm and confident.

The difference between a contract and a favour

One of the secrets of good management is not to allow anyone who reports to you to think that they are doing you a favour. If you ask a team member to write up the minutes of a meeting, this is not a favour: it is a part of their job. However, if you let them think that it is a favour, sooner or later you will run into difficulties; because sooner or later, for whatever reason, the favours will run out. When this happens, strong resentment can take the place of the so-called 'favours' you were given. The main problem with favours is that the contract – or obligation - is always going in the wrong direction.

If someone runs down to the local shop for you to collect your wife's birthday present, they are doing you a favour. They know that this is not part of their normal job description and they know that you are not paying for this 'service'. Even if you are (as owner of a company, for example), asking a member of staff to run errands for you, when it is not a written or even an implied part of their job description, forces an unwanted task on them in a way that gives the employee little or no choice. You might think that you are asking them to do you a favour, but you are not: your are giving them an unpaid task which they can hardly refuse. Moreover, because the employee is doing this as a favour, this implies that you will one day need to repay them in some way. Unfortunately, there is no currency for you to repay them, apart from words of thanks or a salary increase. As a result, you will soon end up in their debt, with all that this entails. If you do something for them related to their work, they will probably see this as 'part of your job' (which it is). If you do something personal for them, you step over the line of demarcation between boss and employee - a dangerous move in any circumstances.

Figure 7 • This diagram shows the inevitable consequence of a manager's inability to give simple orders without making them 'requests for favours'.

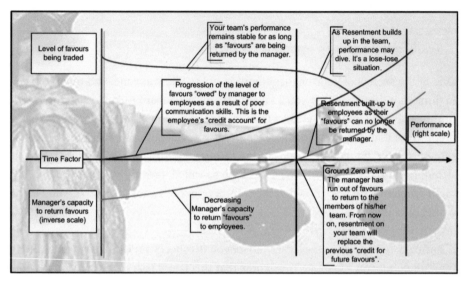

Level of favours being traded

Your team's performance remains stable for as long as "favours" are being returned by the manager.

As Resentment builds up in the team, performance may dive. It's a lose-lose situation.

Progression of the level of favours "owed" by manager to employees as a result of poor communication skills. This is the employee's "credit account" for favours.

Resentment built-up by employees as their "favours" can no longer be returned by the manager.

Performance (right scale)

Time Factor

Manager's capacity to return favours (inverse scale)

Decreasing Manager's capacity to return "favours" to employees.

Ground Zero Point. The manager has run out of favours to return to the members of his/her team. From now on, resentment on your team will replace the previous "credit for future favours".

© Inigo Gutirrez 2007

The golden rule is to never trade in favours. If you want one of your team to do something for you, just ask them to do it – no bribes, no promises. Let them know exactly what it is that you want done and, if appropriate, why, when and with what result. Allow them to negotiate on the timeframe, the extent of the task and possibly even on the quality of the end result. However, once you have agreed all these points, it is a contract. This means that both parties are obliged to honour the terms and conditions.

Negotiation is important for highly individualistic employees, especially those who are not motivated by the prospect of making someone else happy. On the other hand, negotiation should not become an excuse for letting someone talk you out of a task which you have just given them.

A classic example:

THE NINE-STEP APPROACH TO PROBLEM SOLVING

You ask an analyst to make a document outlining the key parameters for a particular problem, saying that you need the document by Wednesday lunchtime. They can negotiate the timeframe: 'Can it be Thursday morning; I have rather a lot on right now?' Or they can discuss quality: 'Can I keep the layout simple – just the key issues? I am rather busy and I would need to research much deeper to give you the actual facts and figures.' This is what I call 'balanced negotiation'. But do not let the analyst talk you out of making the document at all, simply because they decide it is not needed. If someone does not want to do something (because they are either too lazy or too busy), they may be perfectly happy to spend half an hour trying to convince you that the task is too complex or that there are other people in the team who could do it better.

This kind of one-sided negotiation can be avoided if you take a minute to prepare yourself, before asking somebody to do something. Anticipate their reaction or perhaps even ask their advice first. Only tell them what you want after you have listened to what they have to say. You may notice that if you ask someone for advice, things are often quite straightforward, because the person concerned feels needed and is therefore better able to 'understand' the importance of the task.

It is important for an interim manager to maintain a dignified distance between himself and his team. The contract technique described above does not, however, mean that you need to be unfriendly or impolite. I am not saying that you do not need to say 'thank you' when someone does something for you. I am not saying that you should not allow people to carry out simple courtesies for each other, such as opening the door, asking if you want a coffee, etc. However, it should go no further than this. On the other hand, if I see a member of my team is extremely busy, I might say: 'I am going to the coffee machine, can I bring you something back?' Notice that I do not say: 'Can I get you a coffee?' I am not subordinating myself, because I tell them that I am going anyway. Consequently, I am acting as a colleague and a sympathiser.

The problem with the above scenario is that the CEO is creating his own stress. He wants to be liked by his staff as a 'nice guy', but he does not realize how he comes across to them. He is entering into contracts which he can never honour. If he owes his staff a return favour (over and above their salary) every time he asks one of them to do something for him, he will always be in their debt. The result will be that one day his employees will leave, simply because they no longer respect him.

In this particular situation, the CEO needs to make a general rule that whenever a salesperson is sitting with clients, it is the duty of all his front office staff (including himself) to bring refreshments to both the clients and the salesperson. This way, the client gets the comforting impression of a well-coordinated, harmonious company. Of course, this begs the question of the CEO's delegation skills, but that is something he must simply work on. You cannot change your personality but you can change your behaviour - and this particular CEO needs to do so urgently.

Assuming that you have obtained the necessary level of commitment for your project and have all the resources you need, it is now time to begin.

Step 8

IMPLEMENTING THE SOLUTION

STAYING ON TRACK AND KEEPING FOCUSED ON THE OBJECTIVES

Implementing the solution - or 'getting on with the job' - means staying focused, being disciplined, checking and re-checking planning, looking ahead for potential risks, dealing with them before they materialize, etc..

As project leader or interim manager, you have a job to do - and a team of people who depend on you to keep it all running smoothly. They do not care about your feelings; they do not want to know about your hobbies. All they want to know is whether all their hard effort on your behalf is actually paying off. They want to be sure that if someone is slacking, you will do what is necessary to pull them back into line.

A successful project requires clear lines of communication and responsibility. If team members and suppliers are not sure who is in charge, chaos can quickly ensue. It is a sure sign of a confused structure when the interim manager is receiving constant queries about matters which should not really involve him. Delegation is the key.

Whatever your preferred operational techniques, you need to be effective. If you think your project is complex, consider this one:

THE STORY OF THE RESTAURANT

Try building a project plan which reflects the operation of a restaurant. Imagine that you have a dining room to fill, but you do not know how many clients will dine this evening. You have a wide selection of dishes on the menu, but you do not know who will choose what. You have a huge refrigerator full of fresh food that must be consumed within 48 hours. You have a chef, an assistant, a washing-up machine and a waiter.

If each person at each table orders a different meal, your staff must somehow cook all the ingredients and deliver the separate dishes for each course to every table. If too many people choose the same menu, you will either run out of ingredients or have to make the portions smaller, at the risk of disappointing your clients. If too few order a particular dish, you may have to discard the excess ingredients before they spoil.

To add further to the complexity, there is no first-come, first-served policy. The first party may not want their food straight away, while the next one does. At one table a wait of half an hour between courses is fine, at another it is unacceptable. Some clients are easy to please, others are not. Just try planning that with Microsoft Project!

A restaurant is a complex operation, fraught with uncertainties, which few people can run successfully without resorting to frozen ingredients and production-line menus. As a business, however, they have two major advantages: every person gets hungry and wants to be fed; and many clients pay in cash.

If you observe how a restaurant gets its projects (its meals) delivered on time and if you can adapt its management processes to meet your own needs, you will not go far wrong in business.

Some of the things we can learn from the restaurant example are:
1. Good preparation is essential.
2. Tasks do not always arise in the order in which they need to be handled.
3. In busy periods, personnel may need to adapt, by taking on additional responsibilities normally held by someone else.
4. Anticipation and awareness of changing priorities are essential.
5. The importance of creating a balanced and professional team, who communicate well, is of primary importance.
6. Always try to instil the belief that, no matter how crazy things might seem right now, it will soon get better!

THE TRIPLE CONSTRAINT

There are literally hundreds of books on project management methods, many of which are listed in the bibliography. However, the best managers are not necessarily those with the deepest knowledge of the differing methodologies, but rather the ones who can successfully manage the triple constraint of scope, budget and time. Everywhere I go, I always hear about the triple constraint. But what about the fourth constraint: quality? Many methodologies include quality but most companies choose to ignore it as a separate constraint.

Quality is often used as an excuse for not meeting the three other constraints – an argument which I refuse to accept. A good interim manager needs to understand the quality standards of his client and must also be able to clearly explain his own quality expectations to his team.

Quality must be made an issue in all elements of the project, from progress reports and analysis documents, right through to the final project deliverables. For example, if you decide on the format of a weekly report, you should create a standard template for the report, fill one in as an example and circulate it to all relevant team members. Now everyone knows the level of information and detail - the level of quality - you expect in a report. Bullet points and smileys are enough for some people, but you may prefer to have more detail and a personal progress note at the end of each report. This is your way of setting quality standards.

From the beginning of the project you will need to agree the reporting frequency: weekly, twice weekly, monthly, etc. This largely depends on the timeframe and the expected rate of change. For some parts of the project you may need to adjust the reporting frequency. For example, during the feasibility stage, when numerous decisions need to be taken, you might need to issue reports more regularly. In contrast, once you are deep into the development stage, decisions might be few and far between, with fewer update meetings than during the key testing and release stage. In any case, the Project Steering Committee (or Board, as it is sometimes referred to) should always meet at the key project gates. These are the identifiable points when the project moves from one phase to another: for example, from Development to Testing and from Testing to Production.

For progress reporting, I recommend the use of a simple balanced scorecard system to report the status of the project to the Steering Committee.

The 'balanced scorecard' is a clever idea and, if used to its maximum potential, can be an invaluable tool. Unfortunately, the implementation of a balanced scorecard system throughout an entire business structure is difficult. As a result, many companies find that the effort required and the distraction it creates are too great in relation to the potential gains it offers. Yet even a simple version can be extremely useful.

To make a simple balanced score card, go back to the Project Charter discussed in Step 6 and find the list of key project goals If you have not included them, add them now, or at least agree a final list with your Steering Committee. Add them to a PowerPoint slide and mark a large green dot next to each one.

For project assessment, I like to use a green dot, meaning 'everything is on track'; an orange square, meaning 'this is an attention point which needs investigation before it becomes a serious matter'; and a red triangle, meaning 'this is a very serious problem, as a result of which one or more of the constraints has been or will be compromised'. I use different shapes so there can be no confusion for colour blind people or when reports are viewed in black and white. In addition, some overhead projectors are not very good at differentiating between red and orange.

If, at any reporting point, an item meets all of the triple (or quadruple) constraints, it remains on green, meaning that it is on track to be completed on time, within budget and within scope. As soon as the item is definitively completed, you should remove it from the scorecard.

If there is a potential problem with an item, so that one of the constraints is at risk, the green dot should be changed to an orange square. For example, an orange item could simply mean that the purchasing department has not yet placed the purchase order for a product that will be needed in the near future, or that the quality of a deliverable was not satisfactory and needs reworking. In any event, it is something that needs careful monitoring and agreed corrective action. If it is a relatively trivial matter, do not bother your Steering Committee with it - they might come up with a solution that you do not like!

If the status of an item becomes so serious that your planning has been compromised, making it almost inevitable that you will either miss your milestone, overrun your budget, and/or fail to meet the scope or quality constraints, your scorecard should show a red triangle alongside this item. Your original planning constraints have 'hit the wall' and you must consider an alternative strategy as quickly as possible. You will need to consider every available option: make a hole in it, tunnel under it or climb over it. In any event, a radical approach will be required, unless the reason for the red status is considered acceptable and the Steering Committee agrees to re-evaluate one or more of the constraints.

You should not be afraid of red-coded items and never try to hide them. They are a fact of life in any complex project. However, when you have a project item on red, it is vital that you think the matter through before reporting it to your Steering Ccommittee. Even if you do not have a final answer to the problem, offering options is a good way to keep the meeting focused on finding a solution, rather than engaging in an emotional witch hunt. If one or more individuals are to blame for the problem (which is rarely the case, as it is usually a combination of factors that weakens a good plan), you can always deal with them before the meeting , if you have the necessary authority. Alternatively, you should at least isolate them for causing additional problems, thereby minimizing overall project risk. In general, Steering Committees do not expect you to talk with them first, if there is an urgent issue that requires your immediate attention.

AVOIDING SCOPE CREEP

Scope creep is probably the single biggest barrier to getting the project completed, to actually making a difference in the company. It is one of the easiest matters to control and yet it is often completely ignored. Companies with a culture of allowing scope creep, for whatever reason, usually have a poor record for implementing change projects and launching new products/services on time and within budget.

Scope creep should be any project's number one enemy. Ensuring that you adhere to the scope of the project, as clearly defined between yourself and the client in advance, is the biggest part of getting the job done. All requests for changes, from whatever quarter, should be strongly opposed, unless they are considered by *everyone* to be the result of an unforeseen circumstance or offer a definite advantage to the business.

Some product companies fail because they do not establish a clear definition of what they require in their products. As a result, it will often occur that, as project completion for their latest model approaches, some bright spark will come up with an improvement or an additional feature that puts back the delivery date. Sometimes the effect can be so severe that the window of business opportunity has passed by the time the product is finally delivered. As a general rule, rather than trying to design and build the all-encompassing, multi-purpose solution, I prefer to deliver something that is basic, well designed and quick to market. Additional features can always be added later on, once the product has proven itself.

'Keep it simple, keep it smart' should not only be a catch phrase, but also a part of the core philosophy of all good managers. Speaking personally, I am sometimes prepared to negotiate away the 'smart', but never the 'simple'.

Do it now!

'The absolute secret to success is, do it now!'

I first heard this quote more than twenty five years ago – and it has always stood me in good stead. If you want to get something done, don't delay; never put off until tomorrow what can be done today. Make a list of the important things that you need to do at the beginning of each day. Better still, buy some of those small 'Post-it' notes and write a key word or two on each one to remind you of what needs doing. Place them in front of you on your desk, so that during the day you scan them and monitor progress. What has been done and what has not been done? What should be done next? This will help you to focus on the essentials, so that you do not allow yourself to drift away from the things you should be doing. Post-it notes are better than lists, because, like a waiter's order to the chef in the kitchen, they can be moved from right to left in priority of importance and removed and thrown away upon completion.

SOLVING 'INSURMOUNTABLE' PROBLEMS

When the scorecard looks bleak, when a task is nearing red status (if it is not there already), you sometimes need to take your team by surprise and 'shock' them into looking at the impending disaster in a new way.

If time is the main constraint, a good tactic (paradoxically) can be to shorten the deadlines even further. If your team says that they are in serious trouble and simply cannot deliver by the 20th, instruct them to deliver by the 15th. By squeezing a deadline beyond what appears to be realistically possible, you force everyone to think 'out of the box', to look at the challenge from different angles. Desperate situations sometimes need desperate remedies - and the result can often be radical – and effective - new ideas. This method works, but it should not be overused. It is best applied to longer time periods: for example if a delivery date is due in three months, can we do it in one month?

Sometimes, driving straight into a wall is the only way to get through it. If you hit a wall at slow speed, the impact can be painful and debilitating. Hit a wall at full speed and there is a chance that you will pass straight through it. And if you don't? Well, it will be over in an instant and you won't have felt a thing.

THE STORY OF THE TRAFFIC ACCIDENT

A former boss of mine was a brilliant salesman. He could talk his way into or out of almost anything. With his creative mind and his modest ambition, he ambled through life happily. He was an artist by nature and he watched the world (and business in particular) from the sidelines, as if it were a game. He told me the following story just two days after it happened, yet he spoke as calmly as if it had happened to someone else. On a winter morning he was driving to an important meeting in the North of England. It had been raining hard and road conditions were poor. He was a naturally fast driver, so he was already over the speed limit when he entered a dense bank of fog. At first, he could see nothing; then suddenly headlights, cars facing the wrong way and a woman standing in the middle of the road ahead. In an instant he realized that there had been a chain collision and that he was heading straight for a wall of cars and people. At his speed and distance, he could never have stopped in time.

As if time stood still, he made a conscious decision that he would not allow himself to be drawn into the inevitable disaster that was unfolding in front of him. So instead of doing the obvious thing and braking, he decided to keep his foot on the accelerator and look for an alternative way out. It was then he noticed that there was indeed a gap just wide enough for his car. The only problem was that the woman standing in the road was now walking in a direct line between him and the gap. He figured that

---

she would either keep walking, freeze or turn around: he gambled that she would keep on walking. Luckily she did, and he kept driving diagonally across the motorway, aiming to miss her only by a hair, so as not to skid. Without braking, he passed through the gap and straightened the car as gently as possible, passing a fuel tanker on one side and a group of wrecked vehicles on the other. He kept on driving as if in a trance. Finally, after a mile or two, he had to stop because he was shaking so much, overcome by the shock of what had happened. Later that night he saw the accident reported on television. There were 35 cars and trucks involved and the motorway was closed for the whole day. He also saw that the fuel tanker was eventually hit and had exploded into flames.

I am not suggesting that he was right to keep going, without stopping to offer assistance. Nor does this story tell us how we should run a project. But it does demonstrate that if you can keep a cool head, stay focused and look for ways out of problems instead of being blocked by the issues ahead of you, you will be amazed how simply seemingly impossible situations can sometimes be solved.

Engineers often have to tackle complex technical issues, yet surprisingly many of them are not very good at seeing exits or spotting gaps. Quite frankly, they are not properly trained for it. University courses are excellent at theory and applied engineering, but are correspondingly poor in diagnostics training. I have observed this phenomenon so often with software engineers that I have developed a methodology to resolve technical obstacles in as short a time as possible.

The strategy is based upon the following premise: when confronted by a serious problem, most people become overexcited. Adrenaline begins to flow and they experience a kind of buzz. This results in a number of different behavioural patterns. Some people panic, exaggerating the gravity of the situation and painting unrealistic images of imminent disaster. Others become introverted and do little else but mutter: 'I said this would happen; no one ever listens to me'. The most dangerous people in this situation, however, are the 'Lone Rangers', who take unilateral action without discussion – and often without even informing their colleagues.

In the IT world, I have known normally good engineers, who in the face of a crisis have started to debug code or make changes to configurations without recording what they were doing, getting deeper and deeper into trouble. They do not take notes, they do not document their actions and in minutes they can make matters far worse, covering tracks and clues that would have been helpful in making the correct diagnosis. Once, I had to have an engineer literally dragged out of his chair to prevent disaster. 'What are you doing?' I asked, noticing that in the middle of a crisis he was working feverishly on a computer that was not his own. 'I am solving the problem!' he replied sternly. 'But what exactly are you doing?' I reiterated. 'Do you want this problem solved or not? If so, leave me alone; I have it under control!' This is the trademark of a Lone Ranger. They delude themselves into believing that they will be the hero of the day, fully expecting that I will thank them and hold them in higher esteem, perhaps even seeing them as irreplaceable. This is not the way things work in project management. Even if a Lone Ranger does actually save the day, they still need to be disciplined by losing their access rights, until they understand that this method of working is simply not acceptable.

So how should we tackle an emergency? The list below is specifically geared towards an IT (information technology) environment, but it can be adapted and applied to any crisis situation.

The key thing is to put the right questions to the right people:

1. Gather information
   a. What exactly is the problem?
   b. How will we know when we have solved it?
   c. What exactly are the symptoms?
   d. How many people are affected?
   e. What is the real damage to the business (per minute / per hour, etc.), usually expressed in quantifiable impact (man-hours, money, time).
   f. Have we encountered a similar problem before?
      I. If so, when?
      II. Are there any similar circumstances between then and now?
   g. What have we got that is still good (still working)?
2. Begin diagnostics
   a. If something similar has happened before, what was the remedy last time?
   b. What do we have to check to see if the problem is indeed the same? (Do not try to fix anything yet: at this stage you should only observe.)

c. Are we overlooking the obvious?

d. List *all* possible causes; do not exclude any item, however trivial. (This is best done in a brainstorming session in a crisis room and/or via a conference call.)

  I. Next to your list, make a note of what you need to check and who is the best person to check it. The aim is to see whether or not an item is working, so that it can be temporarily excluded from further analysis (generally, you should not be looking for things that are not working but for things that are).

  II. Allocate the items to check between the available resources and place them in a logical order of priority.

  III. Appoint a coordinator. All communication, results and information should be routed through this person.

  IV. Wherever possible, have the team work in pairs, one to do the actual checking, the other to observe, take notes, pass on reports, handle communication, etc. Two minds are always better than one.

  V. Under no circumstances should the groups meet informally to discuss the results of their investigations. This creates confusion, leads to uncharted actions and wastes valuable time.

  VI. All theorizing and discussion should be held in the crisis room, where the appropriate people can listen and comment. The coordinator and/or the project manager (who can be the same person) will then decide on the next steps. They must ensure that the meeting does not turn into some kind of macho debating society, but must keep the discussion focused and upbeat.

  VII. Important questions are:
    1. If we do this, what are the expected results?
    2. What will we learn?
    3. How will we know if our actions are successful or not?
    4. What do we do if they are not?
    5. If we change something, how quickly / easily can we reverse it, if necessary?
    6. Will our proposed actions have a negative influence on any other elements of the project?

  VIII. Keep a strict eye on timing and escalation. Call in resources and put them on stand-by, in case they are needed. Restrict systems access to an absolute minimum; limit it to people who you know can influence the problem environment.

IX. Remember to communicate with those affected by the disaster and let them have updates on a regular and pre-arranged basis. Even if you have nothing to report, be sure to tell them at the scheduled time that you have no news.

X. Agree in advance your communication channels and the frequency of communication. Keep at least one telephone line open at all times for urgent information flows.

I once witnessed a case where a team was busy correcting a major outage, only to discover much later that the problem had already been solved and that the systems were up and running again. Incredible as it sounds, sometimes you can lose sight of the symptoms, to such an extent that you forget what they were or even fail to check if they are still occurring!

The best way to deal with a crisis is to avoid it in the first place. If you have a pattern of crises recurring in your project, it undoubtedly means that something is seriously wrong at the core. In most cases, it is not machines which create and perpetuate these problems – it is the people who use them. If the cause was always as simple as a faulty server, it would be easy to identify and replace, especially if you request the necessary budget in the middle of the crisis.

I once obtained budget authorization for new equipment during a crisis, on condition that it be 'repaid' by the resignation of the person who I thought was ultimately to blame. In that particular situation, the guilty party was the quality manager, who was more concerned about his support systems and his fancy headsets than about solving the root causes of our problem. 'In an ideal world, I wouldn't need you or your staff,' I said. 'How so?' he replied. 'If the quality of the company's software was better written, we wouldn't need the expensive support system you installed!' I made him redundant, kept on most of his staff until the root issues were solved (which took approximately six months) and then I laid them off as well - all except for two, who then comfortably carried out the work previously handled by seven.

Keeping people motivated

During the project there will be days when nothing goes right; days when all you hear are complaints, threats and accusations. On the other hand, there will also be days when things click and the team performs like clockwork. A good interim manager rides the waves, motivating himself and his team out of despondency and back into a positive mind-set.

If a project lasts for more than six months, it is important to organise events and activities to keep up team spirit and allow people to unwind. In general, it is better to follow the team members' own ideas rather than impose team-building activities on them. Personally, I hate bonding exercises, group hugs, survival treks and the like, but if that is what they want, fund it, organise it and take part willingly. Go-kart racing, weekend retreats, getting drunk (if alcohol is permitted) and playing silly games can be fun. Letting your hair down and acting childish releases emotions and fires up the soul. It also gives the team lots of new gossip to share!

THE STORY OF THE COMPANY PICNIC

One of the most memorable events I ever organised was in 1999, the year of the total solar eclipse in Europe. We closed the office for the day, hired a coach and took the whole team, families included, out to an open field, where we had a picnic in a beautiful valley to witness the once-in-a-lifetime event.

When organising events of this kind, it is important that everyone should make a contribution to the activity. In the case of the picnic, everyone had to bring food to share with others; they also assisted with arrangements for music, tables and chairs, games, entertainment, etc. If you simply lay everything out for people on a plate, they quickly come to expect it. And if they don't put anything into the event, they generally don't get much out of it. The best parties I ever organised for my project teams were the ones in warehouses or village halls, where the team was given a blank canvas to decorate and where they could organise all the essentials themselves (choosing the caterer, menu, music, etc.). Through careful delegation and supervision, the team felt that they 'were in charge', while in the background I was ensuring that all the practical details were covered and some much appreciated extras - like champagne

---

THE NINE-STEP APPROACH TO PROBLEM SOLVING

- arrived as if by magic. Sometimes, I also require a financial contribution, insisting that everyone pays a small token fee, although I rarely collect it (and if I do, I generally donate it to charity). Asking people to contribute towards the costs helps to avoid provoking the envy of other, uninvited company personnel.

LONG-TERM PROJECTS

For projects of six months or more, you need to make sure that they are broken down into phases, each phase having its own milestones and goals. These milestones and goals should not just be set for the project itself, but also for individuals. The importance of including people in the end solution cannot be overstressed. When people reach their personal milestones and goals, they also encourage others to do so. By setting personal milestones, the individual is reminded of the importance of their contribution. It also makes it much easier to manage performance reviews and project evaluations.

Some managers like to have performance charts and statistics boards, where people can monitor the progress of the project and its participants. If you adopt this technique, be careful (especially on long projects) that you do not fall victim to what I call 'Church Spire' syndrome. By this I am referring to those 'thermometers' that you often see outside churches, showing the amount of money raised and how much more is still needed to finance the restoration of the spire.

Business improvement and turnaround projects, especially those with slow starts and early obstacles, can make the 'filling' of the church spire thermometer seem an impossible goal. Most turnaround projects are built up from multiple mini projects, department by department. The results of the mini-projects are fed into the global project and thereby slowly into the results of the business. Motivation of team members is very important, since setbacks can have a wide-ranging effect on everyone. Consequently, it is important to focus on successes and make sure that they are well publicised. When it is a group effort, say so. When it's an individual effort, say so as well: don't pussyfoot around, trying to claim it was a team result, when on this occasion it was quite clearly an individual who shone.

In many retail businesses, you will see a notice board with the 'employee of the month'. Sometimes I do the same in my projects, but only when the chemistry is right and people can see that it is intended as a bit of fun. On one project we even had the equivalent of a dunce cap. When a person did something wrong, the hat (a gift from a supplier that nobody wanted) was placed on their desk until somebody else screwed up. Because this particular team was very dynamic, this public 'humiliation' was a source of much humour and acted as a strong motivating influence. Over the life of the project, nearly everyone had the misfortune of having the dunce cap placed on their desk!

Another strong motivation element, particularly on long-term projects, is to try and get the different teams working together under the same roof. If you can find a dedicated room for this purpose, so much the better. Make sure you put up plenty of project-related posters. For example, when the timing of a particular phase is getting tight, write up the 'to-do' lists on large sheets of paper, with the expiry dates next to them. Put the initials of the person responsible for delivering each 'to-do' item next to the date and circle them with green, orange or red, according to their status.

An important point about deadlines: when you set personal deadlines, make sure that both parties have agreed to them. Imposing a deadline that no one believes is achievable and then pasting a red mark to symbolize failure is about the most demotivating thing a manager can do. A deadline has to be a contract – possibly following a tough negotiation, but one that is freely agreed by both parties.

Team T-shirts, sweatshirts and caps, emblazoned with project slogans, are remarkably effective in creating a sense of belonging and group identity, even amongst the most sceptical of employees. If employees and management are reminded of a corporate project by seeing the slogan on T-shirts and other media, it can often help to maintain enthusiasm and momentum beyond the initial launch.

Custom-made project posters serve to reinforce the objectives and the importance of the project. Today, A3 colour posters can be printed in small quantities at a very reasonable cost. Their messages can help to build trends, suggest new ways of working or give tips for efficiency improvements. Although corporate poster campaigns are typically used to encourage cost reduction (e.g. to promote the switching off of computers and lighting when not in use), in large projects you need to allow them to have a more wide-ranging function, so that they can both inspire and amuse.

Encourage a slight air of radicalism within your team. Conformists hardly ever invent anything new, so push out the boundaries and encourage individuals to express themselves. If you have creative cartoonists or art designers on your staff, allow them the artistic freedom to give their own slant to your message. The best campaigns are always those that have the look and feel of coming from the project room floor, rather than from top management.

Like all campaigns, however, it is important to get the balance right. Remember, too, that visitors might see the posters, so they should also be appropriate for external eyes.

At the end of a project (or at significant milestones on longer projects) it is a good idea to award framed certificates, personally thanking individuals for their special contribution. Although, this might seem trite, many people keep these certificates on their desk or office wall for years. Personally, I prefer a big end-of-project party, where personalised gifts are given out by a senior representative of the company. A nice, durable high-quality gift is an effective way to build respect and encourage deeper loyalty. These two emotions are extremely important for igniting the fuel required for future projects and challenges.

Further reading

If you find that the advice that I have given you in this section is not getting through to your team, you can always try: '*One Too Many Projects*' by Geoff Reis and Geoff Leigh or '*A Guide to Project Management Body of Knowledge*' from PMI or '*Organizing Projects For Success*' by Vijay K. Verma. If none of these work, then get hold of a copy of the biggest book on project management that I know - '*Project Management*' by Harold Kerzner - and bash them over the head with it until they shout 'OK, OK you're right, I'll do it your way!'

STEP 9

ASSESSING THE RESULTS

MEASURING SUCCESS BY COMPARING RESULTS
WITH OUR CLIENT'S ASPIRATIONS

If you and your team have done a good job; if the gods of business have been kind to you; if you had the energy and the creativity to carry out your tasks successfully; if fortune smiled on you - then at this stage you should be able to consider the project a success!

Now is the time to compare your actual results with the 'aspirations' listed in Step 4, to see if you have moved a step closer towards achieving them. Along the way, you will have made balanced scorecard reports, tracking your progress through the project, but now is the time for the final reckoning. This is an exercise which requires strength of character. You should be able to review your end results - the deliverables - in comparison with your short-term goals and your long-term aspirations, without making excuses for any failures or shortcomings. This is sometimes much harder than one might imagine.

When assessing the results ask yourself:
- Did we achieve what we set out to achieve?
- Did the project wander off course?
- Is the result delivering what was expected?
- Has time changed the requirements, are they still relevant?
- Are the successes appreciated and understood?
- Are the reasons for the failures, if any, understood?
- Is further action required to put things right?
- What did not go quite so well?
- How could it have gone better?
- How will I do it better next time?

Remember this golden rule: we can learn more from our failures and mistakes than from our successes. Successful people are always being asked to reveal their 'secret' More often than not, their answers are trite, simply because they don't really know. It is much more interesting to ask a successful person what mistakes they have made - so that we can avoid them.

When two sailors read a sea chart, the foolish sailor only sees the wide open stretches of water and the romance of sailing around the world, while the wise sailor also sees the tiny buoys and landmarks which mark out danger and potential disaster.

It is human nature to think that when we win, it is because we are clever; and that when we fail it was because we were unlucky. This makes us feel better and helps us to re-motivate ourselves. However, the satisfaction will be short-lived, if we do not learn from our mistakes.

Man is born ignorant. Moreover, as we progress through life and enter into new environments (school, work, marriage, illness), we become ignorant once more - at least until we have learnt to adapt to our new circumstances. It is our ability to bring knowledge from previous experiences and apply it to the new ones which determines whether or not we are really effective managers. This explains why some individuals who have worked for the same company for many years find it hard to change jobs and adapt to a new employer. The most effective interim managers are those who have had a wide variety of experiences, supplemented by the personal qualities of abundant common sense, good communication skills and strong discipline.

Remember to celebrate your successes and to laugh (or cry) at your failures - but whatever you do, do not ignore them.

Performance Reviews

If you have the task of reviewing an employee's performance, bear in mind that the timing is everything. If a sports coach has just witnessed his prodigy lose a race because he did not follow the race plan properly, telling him so immediately after the race might make the coach feel better. However, it is unlikely to benefit the athlete, who is exhausted, cross with himself and in no mood to listen to criticism, however well-founded and rational. And so it is with employees. Wait until the person is calm and has had a chance to reflect on their performance. Begin by asking their own opinion of their performance and where they could have done better. Listen carefully to the answer, giving positive cues to encourage them to respond more openly. Focus on the areas of weakness where you think you can make a difference, where your advice will be most appreciated and best understood. If they know where they went wrong and if you agree with their diagnosis, concentrate on how you can help them to do better next time.

Sons and daughters rarely listen to their parents. Similarly, it is often better to limit your advice to the areas where you believe the employee is most likely to listen - and most likely to respect you for it. It is not a bad idea to let someone else in the management team give certain elements of criticism, even if you know what went wrong and how to make it better. Focusing on one aspect at a time is usually more beneficial than raising multiple issues. Any comment that begins with, 'By the way you also failed to....' is certain to have the wrong effect.

You must remain results-oriented. If you think that the advice you want to give will fall on deaf ears or might possibly even make things worse, keep your thoughts to yourself. Effective managers quickly learn when to put their own emotions to one side, in order to ensure a better outcome in the long term. Criticising people often makes us feel better, when we are disappointed with a particular result. However, managers are not paid 'to feel better'; they are paid to be professional and to deliver the required results, regardless of how they might feel.

Personally, I think that the sympathetic, dispassionate social worker approach is right - at least some of the time. However, there will be other occasions when more emotion is needed, especially with people who are used to receiving criticism in a direct and forthright manner. If a person was brought up in an environment where criticism was delivered in the form of shouts and outbursts of bad temper, it is possible that your soft, caring approach may not get through. On the contrary, such a person might think that you are actually praising them rather than criticising them.

My advice is only to express real anger and severe disappointment with larger groups of people, the way a football coach might read the riot act to his team at half-time. Within a group, the effect of your harsh words will be more evenly distributed, resulting in an effect almost equal to a stern reprimand issued to an individual.

A good tactic during a performance review is to ask the interviewee to repeat your key points and to ask if they agree with them. Where there is doubt or confusion, take time to make matters clear. Businesses lose many employees through a lack of good quality performance appraisal and objective criticism. Recruiting people is time-consuming and expensive; consequently, time spent in helping to reduce staff turnover is one of the best investments any company can make.

Coping with the hollow feeling of success

It is a sad fact of life that we often feel a sense of disappointment when we have finally arrived at our destination. All the effort and expectation involved in getting there is not matched by the level of satisfaction we experience. Any hiker will tell you that the most exhilarating thing about climbing a mountain is the views that you get when you stop for a rest on the way up. When you reach the top, clouds may obscure the view and the weather will tell you that you cannot remain there for long. You feel a sense of satisfaction, but you know that it will be short lived.

Bob Dylan once wrote, 'You'll find out when you reach the top, you're on the bottom.' A good example of this is the junior office worker who, after many years of hard work and faithful service, is finally rewarded with his first management promotion. However, after the initial thrill, he soon realises that he is at the bottom of a very large heap of managers and that he still has an awful lot to learn about management.

The trick is to accept that this hollow feeling of success is normal. As the poet Kahlil Gibran puts it, 'Your pain is the breaking of the shell that encloses your understanding.' You must dig deep to discover that inner strength that makes you who you are.

An interim manager is advised to take a pause before suggesting a new idea to their client and/or their team. Similarly, it is important for a CEO not to burst into the boardroom on the day after a project's 'go-live' party and announce a dynamic new initiative. His colleagues were also at the party and they might all have a headache. It is wiser to wait for a more appropriate moment, when the aspirin bottle is back in the cupboard and everyone is beginning to make lunchtime appointments again.

When I was a teenager, I once spent the whole summer working in a hot and busy restaurant, washing pots, pans and dishes from eight in the morning to eight in the evening, with my first break at three o'clock in the afternoon. My motivation was that I wanted to buy a Garrard hi-fi record player. The parents of my best friend had one and they were people with style and a deep appreciation of music. In the evenings, they would often sit together listening to chamber music, mostly Mozart or Beethoven. I appreciated quality and knew that I could not afford the very best, but the latest version of the model they had would certainly do for me. And so I worked the whole summer long, earning just enough to pay for the record player, with no speakers, amplifier or other components. When I had saved enough, I took the train to London, bought the player and carried my heavy prize back home. To this day, I still remember the disappointment I felt when I noticed that the quality of the reproduction was not as good as I had expected. My disappointment was doubled when my father asked in near-disbelief, 'How much did you spend on it?!' That was the moment when it dawned on me that the summer holidays were over and that my sun-tanned friends were sharing stories of adventure and fun.

I had failed to realize that I was on the lowest rung of the income ladder, wanting to acquire an item that for many professional adults represented no more than a single day's wages. Nor did I consider that a company sells its products at a profit. This meant that the quality they were offering did not match the effort that I had to make in order to buy it. I had achieved my summer goal, I had hit my 'target', but that single criticism from my father (well intentioned but poorly timed), combined with my own disillusion, taught me a heavy lesson. In future, I would either have to lower my expectations or earn a lot more.

Having learned from my mistake, the following summer I got a job paying three times as much in a family planning clinic, ordering stocks of contraceptives and lubricants (although I was too young to put such things to good use myself). I earned more cash over a shorter period and bought the next hi-fi component second-hand. Thus, the return on the effort I had invested was much higher, allowing me to enjoy a holiday away with my friends, some modest savings in the bank and an amplifier more powerful than anyone I knew had ever owned. I kept that amplifier for thirty

> *years and it only broke down once. Today my son owns it and blasts his college friends out of the house with it. Now that was real quality! It was built to last and nothing about it smacked of compromise.*

As I like to say, 'My hourly rate for an interim management assignment is high, because my client is paying for all my previous mistakes.'

Anyone who has faced bankruptcy knows that they learn far more about business during this extremely difficult period than they do in their glory days. Almost by definition, you only go bankrupt if you make serious mistakes. So to encourage us all, let us consider the following list of famous people, who bounced back from bankruptcy early on in their careers to reach levels of success that most of us can only dream of: Henry John Heinz: (1875), Henry Ford: (1902) and Walt Disney: (1923).

Basking in the glory

'Basking in the glory' is a great feeling; like a moment of pure happiness on a sun-kissed terrace in Tuscany. There is nothing to compare with the feeling of coming first or being a member of a winning team – especially if you are convinced that you played a key part in its success! When we are surrounded by people applauding and paying us compliments, it is unquestionably an uplifting experience. But it also makes us vulnerable. Remember: if people are lifting you up, they are the ones who are keeping you in the air. The moment they turn around to look at the new person entering the arena, they will drop you and you will fall back to the ground - often with a thump.

If we start to believe in our own success and in the compliments we are being paid, we are likely to fall into the pit of complacency. The press like to build people up, just so they can knock them down again and the public seems to enjoy the sight of the rich and famous falling flat on their faces.

It is a strange phenomenon (especially in Europe) that the more financially successful a business becomes, the greater the resentment of the general public towards it. It is almost as if there is an invisible turning point, when public opinion suddenly changes. This change is sometimes triggered by relatively minor issues, such as the aggressive takeover of another company or the publicizing of a few foolish words.

THE NINE-STEP APPROACH TO PROBLEM SOLVING

A classic example of the latter phenomenon is the infamous quote from Sir Charles Ratner.

THE STORY OF RATNERS

'Ratners' was a large and successful chain of jewellery shops, located in every major town throughout the UK. Generations of British customers had purchased their engagement and wedding rings from Ratners. One day, Sir Charles (the young heir and CEO of the family business) was asked a question in front of a large dinner audience: 'How is it that your jewellery is so cheap?' 'Because it's crap!' came the flippant answer. Unfortunately for him, the event was filmed and within hours was being shown on the BBC news. His loyal clients felt insulted that the Ratner jewellery which they wore with pride was, in fact, considered almost worthless by the very man who bore the company name. His public apology was not enough to stop the barrage of criticism and the downturn in the value of his company's stock. Sir Charles was removed from the firm, the name of the chain of stores was changed and a vast re-marketing campaign was launched to try to restore the business to its position in the market before he made his infamous speech.

And the moral of this story?: when you get to the top or have achieved the result you wanted, try not to become arrogant or complacent. There will always be someone waiting for the right moment to knock you off your pedestal.

It is also important to receive praise gracefully and to acknowledge those who helped you to achieve success. This minor courtesy is a good investment in the future - you may have to work with these people again – and can also be useful should things ever turn ugly.

Unless this is your last project, you are going to wake up tomorrow with a new challenge. A good coach knows that it is important for his team to let off steam on the night after the game. But tomorrow is another day - and there is still much to do, if the team is to survive and win again. Everyone will be hungry for a piece of your hard-earned glory. Your competitors will learn from your success; they will follow your example and be better prepared to give your company a run for its money. They may even try to poach your employees. Any athlete will tell you that the effort of staying at the top is much harder than the long, hard slog to get there.

Successful businesses do not focus on the competition and their products: they focus on their clients and their potential client base. They want to know who there clients are and why they have chosen them, instead of one of their competitors.

If your client manufactures MP3 players, their two biggest concerns are probably production and distribution – in particular, making sure that they keep their distributors loyal, not by price margins but by levels of customer demand. If customers are asking for your client's products by name, finding distributors and negotiating margins is a relatively easy task. But if no one knows your client's name or their products, you can offer distributors fantastic discounts and they will still refuse to grant you the slightest favour, if it risks upsetting a preferential supplier.

This means that in business you will frequently come across 'arrogant' companies, companies which know that they are on top; companies whose sales staff do not have to work as hard as your client's company; companies that have better pension schemes, larger reception halls and directors who seem to have all the clever answers that your client's business is lacking. These companies are the Goliaths of the business world. But if you can outsmart them (or if they outsmart themselves), even these mighty giants can come tumbling down more quickly than you might ever imagine. Do you remember what happened to Pan American and WorldCom and so many others? So try not to worry about your client's bigger rivals, but concentrate instead on the market and on their existing customers: that is where the secret to future success is to be found. Focus on current trends and look at the effect on consumers. Can these trends be applied to your client's customers or are they simply short-term fads, which will not deliver real added value?

Some analysts would say that if your client has a profitable business, you should not aim for rapid growth and greater publicity, since this will only alert the competition to their level of success. This will encourage imitation, with their rivals attempting to build bigger and better versions of your client's company, undercutting their prices and stealing their customers for short-term cash gain but without looking out for general customer interests in the long run. This may indeed be true in some cases, but is always true if the CEO relies too heavily on his instincts and does not apply a serious methodology to assess his plans and aspirations.

Conclusion

In business you have no real friends; only team members, employees, clients and suppliers. All you face are risks, threats and opportunities. Do not try and convince yourself that there is anything more to it than this: that would only be an illusion. But the illusion can be fun! *From* business come friends and companions, relationships which can transcend mere commercial transactions and enrich your life on a permanent basis.

Success in business delivers wealth and allows you to choose what you want to do next. Making money need not be a faceless or 'shameful' occupation. When we have financial freedom, we also have the ability to dedicate our lives to the causes of our choice. Each year US corporations and private individuals donate more than 250 billion US dollars to charitable organizations - more than the entire national budget of the United Arab Emirates.

There is no better work than the kind of work that you really enjoy - so I would recommend you to continue in your chosen field as long as you are adding real value to both your clients and colleagues. Or as a colleague of mine once said: 'Man, I love my job!'

PART II

PEOPLE, SKILLS AND GUIDELINES

In Part One I covered the nine steps to problem-solving but in Part Two I offer a more sidelong glance at a number of issues that interim managers are frequently required to deal with. Part Two is more general than part One and does not need to be read in any particular order. However, I begin with personal development, since I believe fulfilling personal potential is the key to everything. Time invested in ourselves is seldom wasted and generally benefits everyone around us. Later, I will move on to specific issues, which I hope you will find both entertaining and useful.

Many of the topics raised can not be covered in sufficient depth to meet everybody's requirements, but I hope that they will bring insights which may provide the basis for further reading and study. Do not forget to visit the www.making-a-difference.be website, since it also contains the 'Manager's Forum' blog, where many of the topics raised in the book are debated in detail. Everyone is welcome to contribute their own feedback and experience.

1. Personal Development

WHO ARE YOU - AND WHY ARE YOU THE WAY YOU ARE?
Your life map

As with the nine steps to problem solving, in order to know where you want to go with your life, you must first look back to see where you came from. A simple way of doing this is by drawing a life map, which details in a visual manner the key events and influences which have helped to shape the person you have become.

To draw a life map, take a large sheet of paper and trace out a continuous S-shaped timeline, with each horizontal segment representing one decade of your life. At your leisure, annotate this timeline with the significant events in your life so far, adding a vertical mark to represent the corresponding age. These events may have been happy (your first date or your college graduation) or sad (an accident, a divorce or losing a job). Think of the people who have influenced you (such as a teacher or some other role model) and the key turning points, where you have seized opportunities or taken important decisions, both in your career and in your private life.

Building a life map is an individual exercise, but it can be helpful to work on yours while a trusted companion is also making theirs, allowing you to later discuss any points which strike you as being particularly important. If you complete the exercise sincerely and in depth, you will be surprised to see why, when and where your life took a certain direction, amazed at how its twists and turns finally brought you to where you are now. Study your life map and you may for the very first time become aware of the way in which long- forgotten incidents actually had a major influence on you. You might also notice recurring patterns, of which you were equally unaware. If these patterns have had a negative impact on your life, ask yourself what steps you can take to avoid them in the future.

Figure 8 • A personal life map

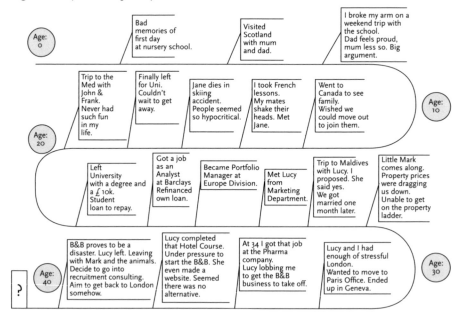

© Inigo Gutirrez 2007

Understanding where we come from and identifying the patterns which have shaped our destiny can help to guide us in new and more relevant directions. By extrapolating our life map into the future, we can begin to see the boundaries and constraints which we may have to overcome in order to fulfill our dreams.

Putting your own house in order

First take the beam out of your own eye, and then you will see clearly to remove the splinter from your brother's eye...
ST. MATTHEW, CHAPTER 7, VERSE 5

When I was a boy, I used to laugh at this biblical verse because. Although I could imagine the pain of having a splinter in my own eye, I could never picture someone with a beam in their eye. Nevertheless, the message is clear: before we can begin to deal with other people's problems, we must first deal with our own. This is only logical: it is not difficult to understand that a troubled, insecure person cannot contribute as much as a serene and well-balanced person. If we are going to lead others and show them the way to improve, it certainly helps if we can consider ourselves to be both happy and successful.

In other words, it is imperative that we work on our own personal situation, in order to ensure that we have our life and career in good order. If our life is out of balance, we can quickly lose patience; our ability to interpret situations correctly is impaired; we become less receptive to new ideas and more abrupt with others.

IS YOUR LIFE IN BALANCE?

At times, your assignments will create an imbalance between your work, your home and your family. As long as you have the continued support of your family and you do not feel depressed about the situation, there is nothing fundamentally wrong with what others might perceive as a lack of balance. However, if you let this state of affairs continue for too long, cracks will begin to appear that can potentially ruin either a career or a relationship, unless they are addressed quickly and correctly. Worse still, the effect of losing one may be so devastating that you end up losing both.

A sad story of a rapid change for the worse:

THE STORY OF THE SALESMAN

I once employed a salesman who had mastered the near-perfect balance between seriousness, joviality and the ability to convince just about anyone to part with their money for the company's products. A year or so later, I was working for another software company, helping them to professionalize their day-to-day operations. Early on in the assignment, I noticed that sales was their weakest area and that very little new business was being attracted. So when I happened to hear that my old salesman was back on the market, I called him in and had the directors interview him. Of course, they hired him on the spot, but I couldn't help noticing the creases in his jacket and his unshined shoes.

On his first day, he joined a junior salesman for a visit to a difficult client. The junior had been trying for three months to close the deal, but each time he returned with

---

another tale of indecision. My salesman not only convinced the client to sign on the spot, but was also able to double the price of the order by adding extra development and support as contingencies! It was the perfect start and everyone was happy – except me. I suspected that he was trying too hard. Had he pushed the client too far? Had he sold something we couldn't deliver? Would it come back to haunt us? On his third day I observed that he was not as cleanly shaven as usual. I had the uneasy feeling that something was wrong. Sure enough, within three months he was out.

He was so successful on his first day, because his adrenalin was really racing, as he tried to prove to me and the world that he could still do it. Inside, however, he was secretly losing a tough mental battle. The sad reality was that he and his wife had split up a year or so earlier (shortly after I had left the company where he worked). He was forced to leave the family home and had gone to live with his father. Three months later his father died of cancer, leaving him homeless. All these factors combined to break his spirit and his lust for life. It was one of the saddest experiences of my career, as I was only too aware that he was sliding down a slippery slope, with little chance of climbing back. His foundations were gone and the insecurity which had plagued him since childhood now gained the upper hand in his life. It proved to be the one obstacle he could not overcome.

Over the last 25 years I have seen many rising stars burn out or fade away, simply because they did not maintain the proper balance between their private lives and their business lives. Some made poor life choices, when it came to their 'significant others'. If you are going to put your career first, you need to be sure that your partner is willing to take second place and accept a reduced amount of support and attention. This may work for the first few years, especially if both partners have a career, but when one of them decides to take the foot off the accelerator or wants to start a family, the first serious rifts often begin to appear.

The daily strain of raising a young family confronts many managers with a very difficult compromise. I have met hundreds of people who clearly decided to put their careers first, phoning home each evening to say that they will be late (yet again). But very few of them would openly admit that they had made such a conscious choice. Somehow they consider what they do to be 'normal' and assume that their families will adapt to it. But what did they specify in their implicit contracts with their partner when they made their life-long commitment? And how does that square with their formal contracts with their boss and clients?

The bottom line is this: if you are planning to pursue a serious career in interim management, there can be no half measures. You need to be absolutely certain that you have the necessary resources and emotional support behind you.

There are three distinct advantages to being a middle-aged or older interim manager:
1. You will have gained much more experience and will be better able to read a variety of situations.
2. Your children will have grown up and should therefore be more independent, even if they have not yet left home.
3. Your relationship is most likely to have matured to a level where you no longer have the constant desire for each other's company and you have become more comfortably independent.

Today, many people postpone starting a family, preferring to climb the corporate ladder to a position high enough to ensure that their chances of maintaining that position, even after starting a family, are greatly enhanced.

Hiring a live-in nanny, for example, is an affordable option for those whose careers are moving faster than the demands of their growing family. I once worked for a CEO of an expanding multi-national company, whose wife was also an international businesswoman. Until they recruited a nanny, it was not uncommon for them to meet at the airport, where the departing partner handed over their three young children to their arriving spouse.

The key point is to understand the need to look after your personal relationships and investments: if you don't, sooner or later it will have a negative impact on your work.

ARE YOU SUCCESSFUL?

How should we define 'success'? There are many different ways, but I am convinced that the only worthwhile measure of success is the manner in which we measure ourselves. If we look back at our career and see that our achievements match or exceed the expectations of youth *and* if we consider ourselves to be 'happy,' then we may also consider ourselves to be 'successful'. However, this definition is far too simplistic for many people.

In my opinion, the only truly successful people are those who honestly think of themselves as a success, who are doing what they want to do, who are earning an income they are content with. By this definition, there is no reason why a bus driver working in the north of England cannot be as 'successful' as the CEO of a medium-sized business in southern California. This argument is not a trendy cop-out: it is an appreciation of the fact that our own feelings are the only ones that truly matter.

When judging our own success, we might be tempted to compare ourselves with former classmates, assessing their job titles, rates of pay, holiday destinations, etc. against our own. This, however, is false reasoning. We may have similar socio-economic and academic backgrounds to our old schoolmates, but their personalities and expectations may vary enormously from ours. One may always be striving for more money, power or fame, while another may be perfectly content with a modest family car and a comfortable 25-year mortgage.

Life partners are notorious for reminding us of our shortcomings. Husbands and wives have the uncanny ability to make each other feel like failures, even when outsiders consider them to be highly successful. If your partner's reminders become habitual, they may eventually bring about the downfall of your relationship - or become a self-fulfilling prophecy. Unless, that is, you are so mentally strong that the criticism to you is like water off a duck's back. But to be honest, I have met few people who are that thick-skinned!

So how do you become successful?

There are five important lists that you need to complete and understand, if you are to make progress with the difficult task of being successful.

You need to know:
1. The things you are good at
2. The things you are bad at

3. The things you like doing
4. The things you dislike doing
5. The ten most important things in your life

Moreover, for each of the lists you need to ask the crucial question 'why'. Why are you good at this? Why are you bad at that? Why are those two hours a week on the golf course so vitally important to you?

Before young managers apply for a position with the Bayard Partnership, I ask them to do some homework first, especially if they show signs of not really knowing what they want to do with their lives and careers. I never accept answers that have not been fully thought through. This kind of wishy-washy thinking may be enough to get them through each day, but it should not form the basis for a career plan.

First of all, I ask the candidates to prepare the above lists. Normally, I prefer for them to make separate lists for their private lives and their business lives. These can be quite different but most often they follow a similar pattern.

Of course, what people write down might not necessarily be the truth, even if they are doing it privately. In fact, I seldom ask to see the lists, because if they are going to mean anything at all, they should remain private (especially list number 5, 'the most important things in my life'). If you are really honest with yourself and you choose to place golf first, your children second and your wife third, this may not be the sort of thing that you want to share! On the other hand, if you are willing to show your lists to trusted colleagues or friends, the resulting critical appraisals can be very useful and revealing. The trouble is that we tend to consult people who are likely to agree with us.

These exercises are not a party game. They are concerned with the basic questions of our lives; the things that matter the most; the things that will help us understand who we are and why we are the way we are.

When you take the time and effort to ask the really difficult questions, this is the first step in the direction of discovering the 'real' truth. It is not something you can do in just a few minutes. At the very least, it should take up the best part of a weekend; preferably away on your own, in a place where you have as few distractions as possible.

A typical list of 'things I am good at' at might look like this:

Table 4 • A summary of good skills

Good skills at work:
1. Organizing events
2. Taking control in times of decision-making
3. Talking with people, encouraging them to see my point of view
4. Bringing order into chaotic situations
5. Dealing with difficult clients
6. Handling suppliers (getting them to reduce their prices and deliver more for less)
7. Making PowerPoint presentations
8. Giving presentations
9. Seeing areas of inadequacy
10. Making plans for the future

Good skills at home:
1. Tidying the house (the children's bedrooms)
2. Negotiating good deals for household repairs and maintenance
3. Planning the annual holiday
4. Resolving arguments and disputes
5. Taking the lead in decision-making
6. Listening to my family, giving advice
7. Food shopping

Sometimes others might regard you as being good at something, simply because you are prepared to do it. For example, a person who is a wizard in Excel will get plenty of analytical work, not necessarily because they are any better at it than their colleagues but because they like - or are willing - to work on spreadsheets.

If you ask yourself why you like doing certain things, the real answer is often linked to your ego. If you conclude that you like to organize office or family events, it could be because you like being the centre of attention or because it gives you the feeling of being indispensable. The thanks and praise you receive at the end of the party is worth all the effort and stress involved.

Understanding the skills and characteristics required for any given profession

A successful concert pianist may be motivated by a number of different factors: by the drive to become the best in his or her profession; by an inspirational love of music; or by the warm glow they feel when they receive a standing ovation at the end of a performance. For them, this brief moment of glory is worth all those thousands of hours of practice. In contrast, many other highly talented musicians never make it, simply because for them the pain is not worth the gain. Even minor criticism can be enough to tilt the balance and put them off performing for life. Consequently, successful concert pianists are a rare breed of people, whose natural talent is more than matched by a combination of ego, discipline, drive, motivation and an arrogance which never allows them to give up or admit defeat. On top of all these characteristics, they also have to be good communicators with a great deal of personal charisma, so as to charm not only their public but also their sponsors and their entourage.

Consequently, a top class concert pianist needs to have the following attributes:
1. massive self belief ;
2. discipline ;
3. ambition ;
4. outstanding talent ;
5. motivation & drive ;
6. strong communication skills ;
7. charisma ;
8. physical and intellectual stamina.

If they do not have all eight, their chances of international success are slim.

In the pop music world, David Bowie is a good example of someone who possesses all eight of the qualities mentioned above. In the mid-sixties, when he was playing in folk clubs in south-east London, people would openly criticize his singing, saying bluntly that he would never make it with a voice like his. 'Don't applaud too loud or he might play another song!' Not many of us have the drive to withstand this kind of criticism. Those who do and who also have the gifts of creativity, originality, vision, etc., are the ones who go on to achieve greatness.

In the world of athletics, the tragedy of failed stars is painfully obvious. Sometimes I wonder how they would have turned out had they chosen a career in business and traded the professional track for a home gym or the local tennis club. However, for true athletes, this will never be an option – at least not until they are satisfied with their achievements or are forced to retire due to injury or some other factor beyond their control. For them, failure is painful in every sense of the word.

To summarize: if managers know who they are and why, it becomes much easier for them to lead and inspire their teams. They can also help others to discover their own unique profile and to perform better by taking on challenges that specifically suit them.

The question 'where do we want to go with our lives' is a vital one, because it is the single most important factor in determining whether or not we will eventually feel satisfied with ourselves. And the sooner we feel satisfied with ourselves, the happier we become and the better we can work.

Your doctor knows what you need, but I know what you want.
BOB DYLAN

You may be wondering whether all this navel-gazing is really necessary. My answer is that the majority of people only tackle these crucial inner issues late in life, usually after much turmoil and pain. It is better to look objectively at yourself and your life every once in a while, rather than waiting for a mid-life crisis before asking: 'Who am I, what am I good for and what am I doing here?'

Life is what happens to you, while you are busy making other plans.
JOHN LENNON

It never ceases to amaze me how many of us have elaborate plans for our future, yet we almost never take the time to plan how to achieve them. Both in politics and in business, forward planning is evolving into ever-shorter timeframes, such as the life span of a parliament or the three-year plan of an interim CEO.

In our personal careers and lives, we need to look at least two to three moves ahead, especially if we work on a project basis or if the nature of our work changes frequently. Knowing what you want to achieve in life is a blessing, because it is then relatively easy to construct a detailed plan to get there. With no vision of the future, too many of us drift on the ocean of life like flotsam, waiting either to sink or to be washed ashore.

Mapping your career path

When planning how to achieve your goals, the secret is not to think in a linear way. For example, if you are young, have no money and you want to become a sound engineer in a top London recording studio, one way into this highly competitive job market might be to work as a salesman for a supplier to sound studios - or at least make friends with one. This way you will gain at least indirect access to all your potential employers, allowing you to find out who is hiring, who is cutting back, who has the big names and which one is right for you. Your contact might even be able to put in a good word for you.

Many people I meet find it difficult to select their career options. Notwithstanding all the education they have received, there seems to be little coaching or advice on career choices. For young people with little or no work experience, it is hard to visualize what a career in marketing or finance is actually like. 'I'm keeping my career options open' is either an excuse by someone who can't be bothered to think seriously about all the possible options or a sign that the person is unable to decipher all the information available to them. People searching for a new career should complete the self-assessment exercises I have detailed in this book and then take the time to investigate what a dream job really involves, in terms of actual work, day-in and day-out.

When I was aged eighteen, finance and law seemed to be the most boring careers imaginable. I wanted to become rich and famous, build things, create things, drive things, run things, control things. Little did I realize that a law or economics degree would have been a better start to realize my ambitions than a photographic diploma or a job pounding the streets as a salesman.

My first real breakthrough was working for a recruitment agency in central London. I didn't know what I really wanted to do, but the job seemed to fit. One day, after working there for about a year, a new job offer came in, which I thought was perfect for me. I applied for it and got it.

The job was working in the busy marketing department of a building materials company in their London headquarters. Although I loved my work, my real ambition was to set up my own business in photography and to combine it with a marketing consultancy. Linking the concepts of PR, copywriting and photography under one roof, I intended to specialize in the building industry.

During the 1980s, there was no digital re-working of photographs and the accurate photographing of buildings was a skilled art. You had to use special large format cameras that were both expensive and complex. The real trick was to understand buildings, to appreciate the details that architects were proud of, and to visualize the photograph on the printed page before you took it. Most important of all, you had to know what time of day to take the pictures, so as to ensure that you had the sun at the right angle, the street clean and the traffic out of the way. You also needed to have at least two strategically placed people to create scale and depth. If you could do all this, you could earn big money. But often it meant standing out in the cold for hours, waiting for exactly the right moment.

The concept for my business was to take great photographs, to write the accompanying texts and to arrange for their publication in the glossy architectural and buil-

ding magazines of the day. How could I achieve all this, however, while working as a junior in a marketing department? How would I persuade architects to give me work, when my portfolio contained almost no high-class buildings?

One night, while away on a company promotional tour, the sales director of the building company asked me what I wanted to do with my life. I told him that although I had been offered a promising career within the company, my real ambition lay elsewhere. When he heard my plan, he asked me how I was going to achieve it. 'You have no money, no contacts, no clients and no equipment'. Of course, he was right. I had a dream of the future, a destination in mind, but I had not worked out how to get there. I had visualized a small office with a small, happy team of busy people. I had thought about company cars, exotic lunches and plenty of travel, with a touch of fame and fortune – but I had not thought about how I was going to start it all off! In reality, I was only a junior employee in a brick company, barely earning enough to pay the bank loan on my house, let alone invest in a business.

The sales director suggested that I switch from marketing to sales. 'But why would a marketing man like me want to become a sales representative?' 'The answer is simple,' said the sales director. 'If you work as a sales rep. for a top brick company, you will earn a lot more money than you do now. What's more, you will be paid to call on some of the best architectural practices in London, if not the world. You will meet some brilliant architects and you can tell them about your real plans. You will need them to become your friends, or at least to like you enough to want to support you, when they can. They will probably offer you photographic work on the side, helping you to finance the purchase of your equipment, and this will form a bridge between being employed and going self-employed.' In two minutes he had shown me the way to achieve what I had been dreaming of for the last five years. 'You're a good communicator and you have enthusiasm for life,' he said. 'Your father is an architect, you understand the business, you have a passion for it and – most important -with some training, you'll make a first-rate salesman - a skill you are definitely going to need if you plan to run your own business.' I was amazed; I had always scorned salespeople, but now suddenly they were the basis of my new career.

I asked him if I could join his sales team and learn from him. 'No way,' he said. 'Our company's products are nowhere near good enough in terms of quality. The top *architectural practices wouldn't give my best salesman the time of day! No, you have to work for Ibstock They are the Rolls-Royce of the brick industry and they have the best reps. in the country. I'll make a phone call for you, if you like.'*

Two weeks later I had an interview with Ibstock's sales manager for Central London; within eight weeks I was on their training scheme; and five weeks after that I had my first luxury company car, a 50 % higher salary, an expense account and one of the best patches in London in which to generate business. Three years later, I had built up a large client base and was doing enough work on the side to go self-employed full time. What's more, I had both Ibstock and my previous employer as two of my top industrial clients.

The sales director in this story was George Gardner, the person to whom this book is dedicated. Thanks George – I owe you one.

Tip

If you have enthusiasm for life, are eager to learn and do not know what to do for a career, go and work in an employment agency, preferably in a big city. The key skills you acquire working for such an agency will be of use to you for the rest of your life.

You will learn how to interview people, to listen to them and to assess them; you will learn the art of sales (persuading companies to place their vacancies with you and not with the competition); you will learn to motivate people to think 'out of the box' when making career moves; you will learn to organize yourself in a busy and rapidly changing environment. Better still, one day you might see a great job opportunity land on your desk – then you just pick up the phone and put yourself forward. By then, you will know that the art of getting a job is to let the interviewer believe that they are interviewing you, while all the time you are controlling the entire process from your side of the table.

2. Interim Management

THE STRATEGIC ROLE OF AN INTERIM MANAGER AND WHY THEY ARE NEEDED

Some people say that interim managers are entrepreneurs, but I don't fully agree with this. I believe that many interim managers would like to be entrepreneurs, or may aspire to be entrepreneurs, or have even tried and failed to be entrepreneurs. In practice, the entrepreneurial ideas of many interim managers do not hold up to scrutiny. Experienced interim managers should be able to recognise, understand and work with real entrepreneurs, but their natural talents should keep them on the operational side of the boardroom table.

Some interim managers are brilliant at identifying the weaknesses of an entrepreneurial idea, helping to work it through until the idea becomes strong enough to launch. But most are simply people who pick up on a good idea and get a kick out of making it happen. I see interim managers as temporary COO's (Chief Operations Officers), logical organisers who use their blend of operational skills and emotional intelligence to transform plans into action. An interim manager can also step in as a temporary CEO, especially if there is a problem that needs solving from the top down. However, once the crisis has passed, they will probably get bored and eventually become less effective, as they find themselves slipping more and more into routine activities.

Keeping the business running in the long term should be the role of the permanent manager. This role should only be assigned to an interim manager for the implementation of specific projects or the solving of specific problems or if the task is linked to a limited timeframe (usually, less than three years; three years is regarded as a long time in interim management, no matter what the project). As soon as the task ceases to be a project and matures into a core part of the business, it is time for the interim manager to recruit his own replacement. Those who stay too long in one place, doing the same thing day-in, day-out, cannot really be regarded as interim managers, but rather as contract employees.

Identifying weaknesses

A problem which many interim managers face is that of working for a business with structural weaknesses that are neither identified nor accepted by the owners. In this case, the strategic role of the interim manager must be to identify these weaknesses, to have them recognised by the client and, wherever possible, to ensure that any imbalance is rectified.

The weaknesses often date back to the very origins of the business and frequently result from the fact that there was never the right balance within the senior management team. In this respect, I am not referring to knowledge or skill sets, but to personal qualities and characteristics. To explain what I mean, here is a catch phrase I wrote for the homepage of the Bayard Partnership's website:

A good idea is not enough; it needs to be nurtured, tested and only then put into action.
HARLEY LOVEGROVE

Possibly one in ten million people have the combination of natural talents to meet all four of these requirements, i.e.:

1. come up with a really good idea;
2. nurture it;
3. test it;
4. put it into action (make it happen).

Most of us have good ideas but lack the patience to nurture them. Nurturing requires you to turn the idea over in your mind, time after time, looking at it from all sides and finally accepting it for what it truly is. For many people, testing is even more tedious and requires considerable levels of objectivity. And assuming that we have completed the first three steps, how many of us have the management skills to handle the day-to-day operational strategies required to put the idea into action?

Many people fail somewhere between the idea and the nurturing stages, but even more fail when they try to bring their idea onto the market. This is usually because they have either not sufficiently tested it or have no real plan for its implementation.

The reason why people are incapable of doing all four steps is that the ideal personal characteristics required for each step are contradictory. This means that unless you have a split personality, it is very unlikely that you will be able to complete all the steps to the standard necessary to succeed.

For example, in order to have really good ideas, you must have vision; in order to nurture your idea to the level of maturity at which it can be launched for testing, you must have patience and focus; in order to be good at testing an idea, you have to be ultra-objective. Unfortunately, vision and objectivity are often the very antithesis of each other - and even if you can manage to be objective about other peoples' ideas, it is difficult to be objective about your own.

Putting an idea into action requires a very special set of qualities which only 'do-ers' (resourceful managers) possess. Doers have a genuine love of planning and a readiness to handle mundane matters (finance, contracts, legal, purchasing, human resources, organisational structures, etc.). They also need the thrill and excitement of solving countless irritating and sometimes trivial problems. They must have em-pathy for all kinds of people and they need enough leadership skills to motivate and guide people through good times and bad. However, they should never dream of becoming the CEO. They must understand that their natural place is number two, a position from where their talents can make things happen without taking over the entire show. A good COO can run the business in times of sickness or in the absence of the CEO, but he will never be able to push it forward in the long term, because the vision required for this task is not compatible with the skills needed for the day-to-day running of operations.

The COO or 'Ops. Man' is therefore the second-in-command. He does not decide where the ship is going or even why, but needs to focus solely on how and when it will get there. In business, it is always dangerous to mix these two roles.

Figure 9 (page 178) outlines the balance of differing elements required to make something happen (the top row) and the complementary skill sets associated with each of these elements (bottom row).

Figure 9 • From 'idea' to 'making it happen': the skill sets required

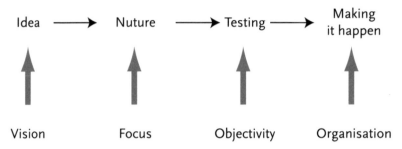

Comment on Figure 9: *It is true to say that you actually need five elements, the fifth one being 'drive'. In my opinion, drive should be present in each of the elements and in every director - otherwise their respective departments will not perform adequately. However, it is important not to confuse 'drive' with the 'driver'. In business, it is desirable to have many people with drive but there should only be one driver - and that is always the CEO. (I have known several companies where the driver was not the CEO, but on closer scrutiny it transpired that in every case it was only the labelling that was wrong: the driver was in practice acting the part of CEO and the CEO was in fact acting in a different role, but using the CEO title.)*

Most successful businesses are structured in such a way that the 'ideas' person is given the necessary space to think up new products and services. The 'nurturing' person takes the idea from the concept stage and makes it ready for testing, by writing the business and marketing plans. The 'testing' person then carries out user surveys, business acceptance tests, impact analyses, etc. And the final stage of 'making it happen' - and keeping it happening - is managed by a structured, efficient and people-oriented operations manager.

Obviously, in many small businesses these distinct roles are shared by a very limited number of people. But those who try to do it all by themselves rarely get their business anywhere near their 'aspiration' level. Some small companies have human resources capable of challenging the CEO's ideas, but this seldom happens. Even if it does, the CEO is often too self assured to listen to criticism, regarding it as 'negative' or 'lacking in vision'.

PEOPLE, SKILLS AND GUIDELINES

Most people would agree that a business needs the classic set of senior management directors: CEO, Sales, Marketing, Finance and Production. Only a fool would imagine that you can have a business without these basic roles being filled in one form or another. However, if the interim manager detects that the four key business elements - vision, focus, objectivity and organisation - are not fully represented in his client's board of directors, he must identify the missing skills and ensure they are all present in all future management meetings.

Generally speaking, the interim manager should be able to cover for focus, objectivity and organisation (these are the talents which make them so valuable), but it is unrealistic to expect them to cover vision, because that is often the one quality that distinguishes them from a natural entrepreneur. In fact, it explains why they are still working as an interim manager and not as a full time CEO.

Today in larger companies, the CEO's job is largely a question of 'keeping the vision alive' and managing the balance between shareholders, employees and clients. Nowadays, suppliers and distributors are usually handled by other members of the management team. Smart companies have learnt that suppliers play a vital role in the success of a business. They no longer see them as necessary components in a chain of production, but as genuine opportunity drivers, working with them in partnership, rather than patronizing them in a 'remember who's got the upper hand' kind of way.

The strategic role of an interim manager is therefore to ensure that the balance between the four key elements in figure 9 is maintained across their client's full range of business disciplines. In order to do this, they must be prepared to deploy their own skills and resources to bring about the required equilibrium.

---

30 SECOND THEATRE: LET'S HAVE A PARTY

The difference between a CEO and a COO

CEO: *Let's have a party!*
COO : *Great idea, when?*
CEO: *Tomorrow.*
COO: *Tomorrow? No, no, that's far too soon.*

> CEO (irritated): Why?
>
> COO: Because we're broke, we're going to need a sponsor, a theme, a venue and a reason!
>
> CEO: You're so negative, why can't we just do it?
>
> COO: We can, but not tomorrow. We'll do it in June, when the weather is fine, everyone is getting into holiday mood, our new product will be ready and we can do it outdoors, so that we can save the cost of hiring an hotel – who likes stuffy hotels, anyway?
>
> CEO: (dejected) Oh God, you're right as always. Just make sure you remember that the party was my idea!
>
> An interim manager should easily be able to take over the role of the COO in this play, but would never be able to replace the CEO, because an interim manager gets far too big a kick from 'getting things done', whereas the CEO hates anything 'logistical' and 'boring'. On the day of the party the CEO will be out front, welcoming everyone. If he is lucky, the COO might get some kind of acknowledgement afterwards, along the lines of:
>
> CEO: (still fired up) That was a great party! We should have one every month!
>
> COO: (exhausted) Over my dead body!

THE TEN ATTRIBUTES OF A GOOD INTERIM MANAGER

Any interim manager knows that you need an almost endless supply of physical and emotional energy to keep pushing the boundaries. He knows equally that this energy can only be replenished if you are not burning up too much in your private life as well. For this reason, the best interim managers are usually people who put nearly all their energy into their work, often to the detriment of their families. Getting the right balance is not something that tends to come naturally to them.

The ten attributes a good interim manager should have are:
1. A strong desire to solve other people's problems.
2. The conviction that they are the best person to solve them.
3. Extreme resilience, the ability to bounce back after any setback.
4. A high emotional IQ.

5. A good memory for faces and names.
6. A clear, structured approach to every task.
7. A natural ability to plan.
8. A strong sense of priorities.
9. The knack of selling anything to anyone
10. A willingness to learn from mistakes.

A professional interim manager must be able to control his mood and present a consistently balanced external persona. If they express anger, it should not be real fury but a calculated display of emotion, aimed at producing a specific result. Interim managers are in many ways like actors on a stage. The difference is that they must remain in character for the entire period of their employment with their client - so the character must feel natural!

Interim managers also need to be sensitive to other peoples' moods. It is important that they have the strength and patience to make subtle suggestions and adaptations, often in busy or stressful situations,. The most direct route is not always the most efficient route; making detours to avoid head-on collisions with people is a necessary part of driving on the road to change and success.

In order to get the best out of his team and to anticipate signs of potential problems (which is essential if the team is to run at a high level of efficiency), an interim manager needs to be aware of changes in his staffs' behaviour. For example (as the story below depicts), if someone who is normally difficult starts acting in a compliant manner, he should not accept this as 'good fortune' but must investigate the strange development further, in order to understand its motives.

THE STORY OF THE TECHNICAL PROJECT MANAGER

During a staff meeting, I once noticed that one of my technical project managers - a private man with tremendous experience and drive - was uncharacteristically quiet. I usually have fiery exchanges with him, but this time he barely dissented when I announced some tighter deadlines. I took him aside after the meeting. 'What's the matter?' I asked. 'Is it something I should know about?' He replied that the day before his mother had undergone a seven hour operation and that during the hours of waiting he and his father had shared a meal and gone for a long walk together. This was obviously a moment in his life when he was forced to redraw his bearings. As he put it: 'Somehow, the things I was stressing over yesterday don't seem that important anymore.' I sympathized with him, remembering how fate had once pushed my father and me together in similar strained circumstances.

WHY IS THERE ALWAYS WORK FOR A GOOD INTERIM MANAGER?

She knows there's no success like failure and that failure's no success at all.
BOB DYLAN

The short answer to this question is because things always tend to go wrong.

It is a plain and simple truth that most businesses go under because the decision-makers fail to recognize that there are serious problems until far too late. Their entrepreneurial instincts override all the warning signals they are given. In business, it is important to take risks but there is a fine line (invisible to some) between calculated risk and foolhardiness. This explains why so many businesses never make it and why so few of the survivors ever become truly successful.

Professional investors build sophisticated models to help them assess their risks. They have business plans and forecasts, spreadsheets and NPV calculations, but they also rely on intuition. If the formal business model does not stand up to scrutiny, they are unlikely to trust their gut feeling alone, but it may tip the balance in a borderline case.

Investors know that there are always more investment opportunities than available cash. As a result, major investors are usually able to 'pick and choose'. Consequently, they are unlikely to invest unless they also like the CEO of the company, even if the business plan is solid and the growth forecasts realistic. Similarly, most investors need to find their investments 'interesting'. After all, the investor will have to sit on countless board meetings and company presentations – much better that he has some knowledge of and feeling for the company's products.

PEOPLE, SKILLS AND GUIDELINES

Pride

Unfortunately, many would-be entrepreneurs believe they know it all: they simply do not want to listen to others, for fear of criticism or for fear of being confronted with unpleasant home truths. Many are too proud or greedy to sell shares for much needed cash or even to heed much needed advice. They believe they must do it all by themselves - otherwise they will have to share their success with others. For many, this false sense of self-sufficiency is an important part of their learning curve and the sooner the entrepreneur recognises it, the better. Once this lesson has been learned, however, the role of the interim manager is given a higher level of importance, because the entrepreneur now understands that the lack of knowledge in his company can be more than compensated by the right choice of interim manager.

Laziness

If you watch a baby trying to take its first steps, it is amazing how much hardship it is prepared to endure in order to achieve its goal. And having taken those first steps, the baby will then expend even more energy to improve its initial results. For the baby, it is simply a matter of survival. In business, the problems we face are often no less critical and tackling them is hard work. However, unlike babies, we sometimes get complacent and tend to rationalize our laziness. We deny the importance and urgency of solving our problems, to the extent that we repeatedly put off today what we assume can be done tomorrow. Many businesses, once they have learned to walk, are so satisfied with their short-term performance that they neglect to invest the additional effort to improve and become more efficient.

Inefficiency

For small businesses, inefficiency is often the killer. The boss runs around like a headless chicken because he fails to utilize his resources efficiently or is too arrogant to let other people help. The common myth held by many entrepreneurs and small business owners is that they are 'on their own'. They grudgingly hire people and only when they feel they have no choice, and are convinced that the newcomers will never be able to do the job as well as they do.

If a business is to make a sustainable profit, it must make efficiency its priority from the very outset. Putting natural talent aside, the CEO must decide how hard he is prepared to work to identify and improve every source of inefficiency. Keeping the business lean and fit is not an option – it is an absolute necessity. The needless wasting of financial and human resources should rightly be considered by the share holders as a serious misdemeanour.

Overriding ambition

Ambition is one of the most basic human instincts. To win a race, to become number one in your field, to accomplish what has never been done before: these are desires which at one time or another fill the heads of all dreamers, entrepreneurs and career-minded people. Babies and children realize their ambitions by adopting an open-minded approach to the solution of their problems and challenges. They learn from their mistakes and sheer determination sees them through. Of course, it helps that they receive unconditional support and praise for every action they get right, and immediate reproach and punishment for every action that they get wrong. In business, there is often very little praise for getting something right and surprisingly little chastisement for getting something wrong. Perhaps it would be better if there were?

Criticism

Unfortunately, most adults do not respond well to criticism. In choosing to become self-employed, most entrepreneurs think that they have become independent, when in reality nothing is further from the truth. They might have escaped their unsatisfactory boss, but they will soon realize that they have simply replaced him with a 'client', who may not always feel inclined to pay his invoices. The newly self-employed often find themselves dancing to the tune of someone who ultimately has much more influence over them than their previous employer! Similarly, a business is dependent on countless external influences, over many of which it has little or no control.

Successful business people learn to play under the prevailing conditions and are always trying to anticipate changes in their environment, adapting them whenever possible to suit their needs. They also learn very quickly to exploit all the resources available to them and to ensure that these resources are working at maximum efficiency, producing the required results. They are perfectly at ease using interim managers, either to replace key members of staff who fall sick or leave unexpectedly, or to execute change projects or correct a temporary imbalance.

Interim managers may be regarded as fortunate beings, since businesses require their services for a whole host of reasons. As such, they are seldom likely to be out of work. However, they can only supply genuine help if they have learned their craft in an earlier phase of their career, by observing first hand how and why things fail. When an interim manager accepts a new appointment, he must identify the company's 'failures' and correct them very quickly. That is his key task.

The nine step approach suggested in Part One is not always intended to be spread over a period of weeks and months. In some cases, the whole process can be completed in a matter of days or even hours. As long as the interim manager is sure that he understands the real nature of the challenge outlined in Step 1, and as long as he is convinced that he has found the right solution to follow, no real harm can come about. If it later transpires that the problem he is tackling is not the most important one after all, he simply needs to admit his error of judgement, stop at Step 5 and return to Step 1 for the more important problem. He can always pick up the initial problem at a later date, if necessary.

Very few successful people (or businesses) became wealthy by pure luck or by never making mistakes. If you find such a person (or business), you will often notice that their apparent success dwindles away very quickly, because the problems they have avoided so far will show up later as serious weaknesses. This is particularly true if they become over-confident in their success and publicize their wealth too openly. In this way, they can attract a great deal of undesirable attention.

THE DIFFERENCE BETWEEN CONSULTANTS AND INTERIM MANAGERS

Long before the days of King Canute, wise men were guiding powerful but less experienced leaders, sharing their knowledge with them and lending advice. In the old days, these wise men were called 'oracles' or 'soothsayers'; today we call them consultants. Consultants can be very useful and most successful businesses employ them wisely. But there is an important difference between a consultant and an interim manager.

Strictly speaking, a consultant only gives advice, making recommendations and putting them down on paper. In general, consultants should be seen as experts in a particular field, whereas interim managers as generalists, who may have specialized skills and experience, but who are best suited to multi-discipline change and project management. In short, they are ready to step in and manage different kinds of business problems and environments. Consequently, an interim manager may be asked to give advice, but their real task is to get a job done.

No matter what I call myself (interim manager, crisis manager, change manager), at the beginning of each assignment most of the client's employees view me as a consultant. To break the ice, I sometimes tell the following joke, which always gets a laugh.

THE STORY OF THE SHEPHERD AND THE CONSULTANT

A shepherd is sitting by the roadside watching his sheep graze on the mountainside when a shiny BMW pulls up next to him. The driver leans out and asks the shepherd, 'If I tell you exactly how many sheep you have in your flock, will you give me one?' 'If you can do it, sure', says the shepherd. The BMW driver steps out of his car and takes out his laptop and connects it to his cell phone, calls up a satellite observation system to scan the mountainside, then opens up a spreadsheet with complex formulas. After ten minutes of feverishly hitting the keyboard, he looks up at the shepherd and says, 'You have exactly 3426 sheep.' 'That's impressive', says the shepherd, as he watches the young man bundle one of his animals into his car.

'Wait,' says the shepherd, 'if I tell you exactly what you do for a living, will you give me my animal back?' 'OK, fair enough.' answers the driver. 'You're a consultant' says the shepherd without hesitation. 'Wow,' says the consultant, 'how did you know that?' 'Because' answers the shepherd, 'you show up uninvited, you tell me things I already know, and you obviously know nothing about my business because that's not one of my sheep you have taken, its my dog!'

This is only a joke, but there is some truth in it. Even if a consultant genuinely does know something about their client's business, they should always remain humble - because as the shepherd instinctively knew, there is a great difference between advising and doing. Good advice is only good if it is welcome and if it can be implemented.

An experienced investor once told me that he never invested in businesses run by ex-consultants, because consultants are too theoretical. Generally, consultants spend their professional careers giving out advice, without any real commitment to follow that advice through. As a result, when it comes to putting their own ideas into practice, many of them fail - simply because they lack the necessary implementation skills. What might look easy from a distance, can often be surprisingly hard to do.

If you need advice or want to know what your business is doing wrong (or should be doing right), go to a consulting firm. But if you want to implement something or change the way you do things, you should bring in an interim manager. You might be lucky to find someone who has both the knowledge and the ability to take his jacket off and get the job done.

CRISIS MANAGERS AND INTERIM MANAGERS

A crisis manager is an interim manager who specialises in turning around desperate situations and actively seeks them out, often demanding result-related bonuses and fees commensurate with the risk involved.

Although I hear much talk about bonus-related assignments, they are still relatively rare, mostly because of the complexity of policing them. At the end of an assignment, it is surprising how quickly the euphoria of success dies out, if the legal and finance departments of your client step in to renegotiate the bonus scheme which seemed so watertight at the start! I avoid this type of assignment whenever possible, preferring a professional hourly fee on a 'best-effort' basis.

An interim manager may on occasion handle a crisis, but it is not their primary field of expertise. Fortunately, most interim managers are not usually faced with immediate crisis situations when they take up their appointments on day 1. However, unless they tackle their challenge quickly and efficiently, the situation may well develop into one.

In order to explain my approach to the first 48 hours of an interim management assignment, I have invented an imaginary business that is, in fact, an amalgamation of three actual businesses I have worked for in the past as an interim manager.

Each of the businesses had fewer than 150 direct employees; each was active in the field of high-technology computing or software; and each was looking to achieve increased profitability and rapid growth, in order to meet the expectations of their investors.

It is also relevant to note that two of the three companies were less then honest about the seriousness of the situation for which I was brought in. One, in particular, went to great lengths in order to hide the true financial position from me. I have called this fictional company 'Datatronics'.

Key activities during the first 48 hours in Datatronics:

1. Understanding exactly why I am needed.
2. Does the situation as explained by the company match my immediate experience of it?
3. Encouraging colleagues to 'speak truth to power'.
4. Checking the key indicators of truth:
    a. Organisation charts
    b. Bank balances
    c. The 'real' cash flow – how much time do we have?
    d. Sales figures versus invoices versus credit notes
    e. Outstanding invoices – client satisfaction (renewal of support contracts, etc.)
    f. Readiness of products in R&D: evidence of project planning and slipping budgetary controls, etc.
    g. Proof of concepts – early trials, client opinions
5. General indicators of truth:
    a. Toilets
    b. Age of cars in the car park
    c. Clutter in the hallways
    d. Nervousness on the work floor

6. Identifying the right contacts, to obtain a 360° view on the business.
7. Understanding the fundamental internal politics.

Understanding the Need

Before any serious checking and confirmation of information can take place, I feel that it is important to establish a Departure Point. The Departure Point is normally a short description of the current situation (from the standpoint of the person who has briefed you) and takes the form of a simple statement, which can sometimes be supported by a simple graphic illustration.

For Datatronics the Departure Point was as follows:

Datatronics has developed its own range of software tools to help their clients manage their corporate data in a more efficient way. The tools took longer to develop than expected and the directors have won agreement with the shareholders to invest an extra two million euros (expected to arrive on the bank account within six weeks), in order for the company to recruit a Marketing Manager and to put the sales strategy back on track. The overall objective is to be sure of hitting the sales target originally planned for the end of December 2001, at the latest by the end of June 2002.

My role as Interim Manager is to act as stand-in COO, managing the software development process, aligning production with the Sales and Marketing departments and doubling up as Marketing Manager, until the new person is recruited.

From this Departure Point the assignment can begin.

But a problem remains: 'What does my client expect from me?' and 'What does he need from me?' In order to be awarded this assignment, either I must have sufficiently impressed the client during our interviews or my reputation must have done 90% of the work for me in advance. I have listened attentively during the briefings, made plenty of notes and created a huge list of questions. However, it is absolutely vital to be sure of what the client requires of you. Far too often the client has an unrealistically high expectation of what I can do (my success stories, coupled with glowing testimonials and a high daily fee, may all suggest to him that the assignment will be a 'walk over').

This overly ambitious outlook often results in the client oversimplifying important issues, not bothering to give me what he considers to be 'irrelevant' information. As the new interim manager, it is important that I don't shoot myself in the foot by making the same mistake of oversimplifying the problems or being too impressed by my own past successes. From now on *all* information I receive must be treated with an open mind, skepticism and a degree of disbelief. This is the contradiction with which all interim managers have to live and work. The success of the interim manager in extracting and correctly interpreting the relevant data is the key factor along the road to assignment success.

Matching the 'explained situation' to the reality

There are three important questions which you need to ask yourself: Is what I am being told true? Do I believe it? If not, why not?

Early on in the Datatronics assignment, I looked for obvious signs of possible mismatches or hidden truths in the statements contained in the Departure Point. The CEO had told me that he didn't really need a COO, because his secretary was running a 'very tight ship'. In fact, it was only because it had been suggested by the Shareholder Board of Directors that he decided to bring in a COO at all. These statements seemed at odds with reality. When I walked around the offices, I noticed that there were often empty boxes lying around; in-trays were overflowing; the average number of unread e-mails per person was rather high; the toilets were not cleaned properly; and the extra toilet rolls were simply lying in a box on the toilet room floor. Moreover, when you phoned the company it took a long time to get an answer, and when you eventually did, it was often by someone unqualified. This did not look like a 'tight ship'.

Once I had discovered this habitual pattern of over-optimistic truth, I soon came to realize (what everyone else in the business knew for a fact) that this was a trait of the CEO. Consequently, it was not unreasonable to assume that his over-optimism might well have permeated the entire business, so that people were afraid to openly admit what they inwardly felt.

This was an urgent situation and most of the employees were nervous about their future. They were keen to show me that the current troubles were 'not their fault'.

Nevertheless, a quick look at the reporting procedures gave me a very clear indication of the inaccuracy and inadequacy of the company's internal flow of information. A severe lack of formal reporting procedures, combined with minimal feedback and responses, meant that nothing was reliable. It seemed clear that this state of affairs had grown directly as a result of the fact that the company was generally mismanaged (a situation not helped by the fact that it had grown too quickly, through overinvestment rather than financial success).

This was one of the strangest and most worrying features I noticed at Datatronics: very few people were actually 'managed'. Nobody's actions were closely followed up. Positive encouragement was not balanced by constructive criticism. In fact, everyone was more or less left in peace, allowed to get on with whatever they thought they needed to do. This placed me in a difficult position, since it meant that nearly all the information I received was 'partial' (given by the member of staff concerned) rather than being 'impartial' (provided by a supervisor). This made verification difficult, since there were no weekly reports or meeting minutes for me to fall back on.

Other interesting mis-matches I noticed were:

1. *Organization charts:* When I asked the CEO to sketch one for me, it did not match the one I had seen on the company's intranet site. More importantly, when I asked other employees to draw up their own version of the organization chart (in particular, who they reported to and who reported to them) the results were nearly always different from those provided by the CEO!
2. *Sales figures:* The 'back of an envelope' figures which the CEO had given me during our first meeting did not match the actual sales invoices. Most revenue was not coming from the sources defined in the sales strategy but from other non-product related sources (customized developments etc). In Datatronics, more than 40 % of the sales were 'peripherals' (such as pieces of hardware and training) and not actual software licenses.
3. *Client satisfaction:* I noticed that there was an unusually high number of credit notes. The normal percentage of clients buying support licenses at the end of the first year was also very low. Often the licenses were offered to them free of charge or at an unrealistic low cost.
4. *Costs:* The CEO's estimation of his actual monthly burn rate was far lower than reality. When I challenged the difference, he immediately admitted that he had

forgotten to include the cost of the company cars and the leasing contracts of the computers. (Later on, I realized that he simply had no idea of what was really happening in his company and that he had not bothered to really monitor it, since the first few sales orders had started to come in.)

If you are lucky, the company's explanation of the situation will match the actual reality, but experience has taught me that this is often not the case. No one likes to be told they are lying or doing a bad job, so the interim manager needs to absorb all the facts but *not comment* at this very early stage.

Of course, during the first 48 hours it is only possible to gain a rather superficial impression, because the interim manager must not allow himself to be seen as an auditor. If he does, he will never win the complete and utter trust of his management colleagues, which is so necessary for the success of his mission. Instead, he has to be subtle with his questions and not link too many together in an obvious chain. Asking the same question to different people without them knowing gives a much broader insight into the general position and is a good indicator of how much work will be involved in getting to the truth - and thus coming up with a workable course of action.

In 48 hours it should be possible to understand the basic financial situation of the company (assuming that fraud can be ruled out). However, the key success factors for turning around a failing business are more concerned with generating strategic focus and efficiency. The data you need to tackle these matters is complex, often contradictory and challenging. Consequently, the first 48 hours are critical for gaining trust and belief. Everything – I repeat, everything - you do during the first 48 hours should encourage people to believe that you are the person who can help to turn all their hard effort into success.

IDENTIFYING REPETITIVE PROBLEMS

Repetitive problems require special attention. When problems have a habit of recurring, notwithstanding persistent attempts to resolve them, this can have a damaging effect on staff morale, not to mention all the wasted effort involved. Only a foolish interim manager would immediately suggest 'quick fixes', when in reality caution and a much deeper analysis are required. Of course, it is only through experience (trial and error) that we learn, but repetitive business problems are often linked to behavioural patterns of senior management.

A good example of this is the small company that repeatedly experiences cycles of severe cash flow problems.

THE STORY OF THE RECORDING STUDIO

Imagine that you have a successful recording studio business, with a good stream of clients (mostly generated from advertisements in music magazines, press articles and support advertising from equipment suppliers).

Everything is going well, except that your business is cyclical (not so many people record albums in the summer). Even so, if you spread your income and costs over a 12 month period, the result is a reasonable profit from which you can live quite comfortably.

However, you have four key weaknesses:
1. *You get bored easily, especially with administration and prospecting for new projects. You pay other people to do this work, which in theory you could do yourself, but can't be bothered.*
2. *You have a deep fascination for studio recording equipment and cannot resist buying the latest and most expensive gear (convincing yourself and your colleagues that it is the fully equipped studio which makes you 'so successful').*
3. *You are bored with recording mundane local bands and only want to record the best, so you are always looking for schemes to 'enhance' your business - and your life style. (When you do not have artists who inspire you, you tend to spend more time at home or take holidays with the kids.)*
4. *Personal image and self esteem are the key drivers in your life. You are motivated by people praising you, especially those who are rich and famous. Consequently, you take any kind of criticism very hard. Only the best will do for you. You like to spend money on clothes, cars and other accessories that separate you from your competitors – and the crowd.*

The combination of the above four weaknesses has the potential to destroy a perfectly good business, especially if the key actor becomes lazy or ill. A good revenue stream can dry up very quickly. If a business of this kind is supported by bank loans, credit cards and other debts, it can fold in a matter of weeks or months, once the creditors realize the seriousness of the new situation. Some people only manage to avoid impending bankruptcy by selling off tools and other assets, which need to be replaced when new orders come in.

In these circumstances, you are likely to end up with a cycle which will create repetitive cash flow problems. No sooner do you win more clients or receive praise from a new client, than you immediately feel that matters are on the mend and therefore start a new round of investments on borrowed money.

This type of cycle is just one of many, but it can easily be adapted to a whole range of other scenarios (for example, when every time a company wins a large order they feel confident enough to take on extra sales personnel, etc.).

Figure 10 • A repetitive cycle

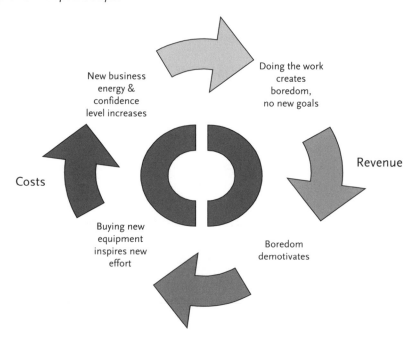

New business energy & confidence level increases

Doing the work creates boredom, no new goals

Costs

Revenue

Buying new equipment inspires new effort

Boredom demotivates

To conclude: when taking decisions, you need to consider the personalities of the dominant figures in the business. If you recognise repetitive patterns, dealing with the core issue is the only way to solve the problem once and for all.

3. MANAGING PEOPLE

CONSIDERING TURNOVER (THE LOSS OF TEAM MEMBERS AND STAFF)
(See also the section on recruiting in Step 7 of Part One)

If you have a pattern of not being able to retain staff, the source of the problem is sometimes to be found at the selection and hiring phase. At the interview presumably everyone was happy and looking forward to the future. As the employer, you believed that the new recruit would succeed where his or her predecessors had failed. The new employee may have thought that this was the major turning point in their career. So what went wrong?

If you need a train driver for your project or business, you must make sure that you do not recruit someone who likes to interact with people and prefers to work in a flexible environment. They might keep it up for a short time, providing you offer the necessary levels of motivation and support, but at some point they will snap, leaving your train stranded miles from the nearest station.

On the other hand, if you need someone who is creative, who can think on their feet, adapt very quickly and is ready to accept change at short notice, you will not want a train driver but an events organizer.

There are two common errors in interviewing and negotiation: the first is not asking the right questions and the second is not listening to the answers. You will be astonished how often interviewers forget to ask even the most obvious questions. For this reason, it is important to remember to always ask the key basic questions, such as 'What are your real expectations from this job' and 'What are your career hopes for the future?' The answers to these questions can give you a useful indication as to where the candidate is heading and whether or not he/she might fit in with your five year plan. Make a list of the questions that you should ask and use it as a guide if the interview gets stuck.

If you ask the right questions, you at least stand a chance of obtaining the information you require. However, I have also met many people who know how to ask all the right questions, but who only listen to the answers they want to hear.

Of course, you know in advance that the interviewee is going to say whatever they think you want to hear. However, by creating the right environment and with the right kind of questioning, you should be able to find out if your interviewee's agenda is different from your own. If there is no synergy, it is better to say so right away: do not assume that you will be able to pull them around. This advice applies equally to all aspects of business life, such as negotiating deals and prospecting for new clients. It has become an overused expression, but looking for a 'win-win' situation is the best thing you can do. Agendas may differ, but if the goal is shared and a proper synergy is in place, the prospects for a fruitful collaboration are good.

As we discussed in Step 7, the leader with the best team stands the best chance of winning the game. Whereas wealthy companies can afford to recruit the best staff, cash-strapped businesses need to recruit wisely, because hiring mistakes can cost them dearly.

> **Tip**
> *The right junior at the right time with the right coaching (often under the guidance of a part-time, highly qualified interim manager, who the junior will not see as an obstacle or threat to his career) can have a major positive impact on a small business – but you have to understand the candidate's long-term career strategy and evaluate the risks of them leaving too soon. You should even try to anticipate it before they are aware of it themselves! If you have a brilliant young salesperson, you know that it won't be long before one of your competitors set their sights on him. Consequently, it always helps to pre-empt these situations and to have a plan in place - just in case.*

The unwanted loss of an employee or team member is one of the most serious but also one of the most 'avoidable' problems in interim management. Apart from adopting the right recruitment methods, you need to ensure that you employ the right motivation for your staff, with a system of adequate loyalty programmes and an attractive company culture.

Problems of this type most often come to light when a manager asks for and 'expects' a result from a particularly difficult employee or team member. The short dialogue below demonstrates this point and hopefully offers a few pointers as to where the basic issues lie. It is a dialogue between a project manager (PM) and an engineer:

---

30 SECOND THEATRE

Time reports

PM: *When can I have your weekly report?*

Engineer: *What do you want: the finished software or the weekly report?*

PM: *It is not a question of what I want, but what I need - and I need both.*

Engineer: *Well, I just don't have time for both.*

PM: *Now tell me, is this a problem of personal time management or is the planning that we both agreed, only last week, already flawed - and if so, how?*

Engineer: *Look, I have just been dumped a load of work from the network team and I need to get that finished by Friday, otherwise the whole system goes down...*

PM: *OK, in that case you need to focus on completing your weekly report, in which you can point out that your workload has unexpectedly risen and is now impinging on your promise to deliver what we had agreed. Then I can begin acting on your behalf to clear your backlog!*

Engineer: *All I need right now is some space to get on with the really important stuff that needs doing!*

The key questions here are whether or not the engineer is choosing his own priorities and whether or not the network team has more authority than the PM. In either case the PM has work to do. Nine times out of ten, incidents of this kind are really about the PM establishing his authority, rather than a difficult engineer.

In my experience, a PM who can exercise discipline, coupled with pragmatic time management, is someone to whom so called 'difficult' people generally respond well. The key point is that everyone is different - and the way you treat one person may differ widely from the way you treat another. However, if you are the PM, you must not allow yourself to become the victim of the situation. Consequently, you must ensure that you are seen to be taking the final decision, in conjunction with your management colleagues. In the case above, this means the manager of the network team.

FIRING PEOPLE

'Being fired' or 'made redundant' are more or less the same thing for the person on the receiving end, even though technically speaking 'firing' refers to the removal of someone for poor performance (so that the person will be replaced), while 'redundancy' applies to those who are dismissed because the company can no longer afford to keep them or no longer needs them (and therefore will not be replaced). In either case, the person is likely to feel rejected, cheated or a failure. The one thing I have learned over the years is that it is impossible to predict how someone will respond in this situation. Although most are reasonably compliant, everyone is unique and every kind of reaction is possible. To a large extent, this depends on the way in which the dismissal is carried out.

Companies often get someone else to do their 'dirty work' for them. An external consultant or interim manager is considered ideal for this task, because it allows the company to hide behind excuses and pass on the reasons - and the blame - for the dismissal to the 'outsider'.

The need to make someone redundant and even the need to fire someone should be viewed primarily as a failure on the part of the employer, not on the part of the employee. In most redundancy cases, you could argue that the fault lays with the optimistic plans and business forecasts of the management, which could not be met in reality; or that the company failed to react quickly enough to market trends; or that sales revenues fell short of expectations; or that costs flew out of control: the list of possible reasons is almost endless. In the case of someone being fired, the cause might very well be traced back to ineffective recruitment procedures, inadequate training or poor motivation. Whatever the reasons, the company's human resource management team should look closely at their own role in the matter and accept their share of the blame.

No one should ever enjoy dismissing people. If you have never been dismissed yourself, you can have no understanding of the emotional impact it can have on the individual. This is never more evident than in cases of downsizing, where employees were recruited by charismatic HR managers and sold stories of fast growth, riches and fame, only to discover that one year later the company is now going rapidly downhill, the CEO is nowhere to be seen and the basic commercial principles upon which the business was founded no longer exist. If the employees in question have worked doubly hard during recent months, doing their best to keep the company afloat, the sense of rejection will be even greater – even if they knew the outcome was almost inevitable.

If you must fire someone, do it with compassion and respect. You should show as much dignity as possible to the individual in question and always have someone else in the room to act as a witness – they need not say or do anything, but should be there to observe what goes on and to assist in calming the person, if they become emotionally upset. They can even call for help in the unlikely event that the person becomes aggressive.

I have fired hundreds of people in my career and on only two occasions have I had potentially difficult situations. I have had some employees literally beg for their jobs back, offering to work for lower wages, promising all sorts of changes in their performance. In all such circumstances, it is essential that you say as little as possible – tell them only what needs to be said, repeat it several times if necessary, but never change your mind or offer a compromise of any kind. You went into the room with a task in mind and you need to come out of the room with the task accomplished. Anything else would be bad for all concerned (including the other employees). This is an unpleasant part of any manager's life but it is also an integral part of that life: especially if the manager is an interim manager. Due to the nature of our work, it is highly likely that an interim manager will end up doing more firing than hiring in the course of his career. But that is what we are paid for.

Surprisingly, even people who are recruited for specific projects show very similar symptoms of rejection at the end of their contracts. Project workers know in advance that the end of the project means the end of their employment but if the project has been fun and has delivered the desired results, they may still feel a sense of betrayal and loss, particularly if some project team members are kept on afterwards.

When making people redundant and or firing people for (relatively) non-serious reasons, it is not advisable to give detailed and specific justifications for your actions.

Confine yourself to the basic details and do not enter into discussions that could lead into negotiations or arguments of any kind. Do not point out all the things which the person has done wrong; but simply thank them for their efforts and explain that their skills and services are no longer required in the new structure. The aim is to get them out of the building as quickly as possible. Always give them the opportunity to call you back later, should they have additional questions. These rules, however, are not applicable when people are fired for gross professional misconduct or for other serious reasons. In these cases you need to take specialist advice, since every situation is different and may involve liaison with external lawyers and/or the police. These situations cannot, for obvious reasons, be covered in a book such as this.

In the unlikely event that the fired employee does phone you back after a few days, try and say no more about the reasons for their dismissal, but simply ask how they are getting on and if they require any help in finding new employment. In European countries there are agencies and support groups to assist them and you should have details of these organisations or at least refer the person to your personnel department for advice. Once again, under no circumstances should you give them any false hope for the future; this is not fair on them and will always rebound back on you in due course.

Many interim managers are required to fire people who live within a relatively short distance of their homes. This means that there is always a chance that one day you will bump into people you have fired. I was once in a restaurant, enjoying supper with an important overseas client, when I was suddenly confronted by a very angry (and drunk) woman whom I had fired a year earlier. I tried to calm her down without causing a scene and luckily the restaurant owner came to my rescue, escorting the woman to the door.

On a more positive note, I can also recall more than one occasion when people have thanked me for the opportunity I had given them, even though I had just fired them! In this respect, having a distinctive family name can be both an asset and a drawback. My mother once told me that she had a student in her adult art class, who asked if she was related to me in any way. When the student learned that her teacher was indeed my mother, she went on to say what a wonderful boss I had been and how she had learned so much from me, and that she was now a department manager in a national bank. I was quite surprised to hear this, because I had fired her in rather difficult circumstances many years earlier. However, she told my mother that she had learned from her mistakes and had moved on with her life. It is nice to know that some stories end happily.

Tip
The best way to fire someone

1. *Be certain of your ground. Do not begin the process unless your mind is fully made up, but do not delay a decision because the act of firing is unpleasant or because of the personal circumstances of the individual – these factors should have no impact on your actions.*
2. *It is important to remember that the way you treat people in these situations will be widely reported both inside and outside the company. When someone is fired, it is unlikely that they will speak highly of either the company or the person who did it to them. No matter how you carry out the task, colleagues, family and friends will always be upset and believe that it could have been handled better. Firmness and dignity are the two key rules.*
3. *You and the team involved need to show discipline: there is an unpleasant task to do and it must be carried out with as little fuss as possible.*
4. *Communication. Prepare in advance what you are going to say to his or her colleagues, when you will say it and how. If at all possible, play the issue down. Even if the person is being fired for a very serious reason (such as corruption), you only need to communicate the bare essentials.*
5. *Timing. If the person is still in their trial period, do not leave the bad news until the last minute of the last day. If you know in advance that you are not going to extend their contract, move quickly to get it over and done with. This is best for everyone. Do not mislead people or give them false hope: it not only creates needless distress for both you and the person concerned, but also for other colleagues, who are most likely waiting for the management to make a decision. If you have the choice, do it early in the week. Tuesday afternoon has been shown to be the best time. It gives the dismissed person time to regain composure and contact employment agencies during the week, before they have to face their family and friends at the weekend.*
6. *Secrecy. Never tell other colleagues before the person concerned has been informed. Everyone in this unfortunate situation has the right to be the first to know. The only other people you need to inform are those who authorized the decision, security (in case of problems) and the IT department, so that the person's access to information*

systems can be limited or removed during the dismissal interview. Do not remove access beforehand, unless you are certain there has already been a security breach.

7. *Keep the dismissal meeting short and to the point; do not let it turn into a long discussion or argument. Under no circumstances engage in debate or any kind of negotiation. The time for such matters is long past.*

8. *Containment. Remove the person from the building as soon as possible. Do not let them wander around the premises unescorted after the interview is completed; someone reliable should be with them at all times. Have a box handy, so that they can clear their desk and collect their personal belongings.*

9. *Offer them a taxi, if you think that they are not in a fit state to drive home. If you are retrieving their company car, have someone drive them home, so they can empty their car in privacy, without everyone looking in the company car park.*

10. *Honour any agreement that you have offered, immediately and without hesitation.*

NICE MANAGER OR TOUGH MANAGER?

Over the years, I have met managers and directors who are frightfully unpleasant to their subordinates. Supposedly, their only concern is for the interests of the business, but in reality they are really concerned about themselves. They will do anything necessary to achieve the impossible targets which their superiors have set for them - or, even worse, to achieve targets they have set for themselves. The trouble with such managers is that they have no respect for the feelings for others. However, they forget that some day they may badly need the assistance of the very people who they are now treating so shamefully. And it is only to be expected that these people will not lift a finger to help. There is nothing more pathetic than a thoroughly obnoxious manager pleading for assistance, like a fallen dictator whose 'friends' have deserted them.

Often the profiles of tough managers are hand-picked by directors, new to a board, who want to make an immediate impact. They recruit tough people who are prepared to slash operating costs by whatever means it takes. This type of person has few or no scruples: if they found out that a sub-contracting firm selected by them was using child labour to assemble their products in unsafe conditions, they would justify it with self-serving arguments such as: 'If we don't employ them, someone else will.' Ethics in business are an important topic, which I am unable to address here, except to suggest that in every aspect of our lives - personal and professional - moral codes of conduct are vitally important. In senior management, the decisions we make have an impact on real people, and so we need to ensure that we can live with these decisions, no matter how tough they might need to be.

THE STORY OF THE BANK TRANSACTION

I once worked for a company which had a bank on its premises, so that the staff could avoid the need to drive into the nearest town. The bank office was small, allowing only one client at a time. I was sitting at the bank clerk's desk and, admittedly, the transaction was taking longer than I had hoped, when suddenly there was a loud knocking at the door and an angry voice shouted: 'Hurry up!' When I had finished, I opened the door and calmly asked the person waiting outside (who later I discovered to be a senior manager) why he had banged on the door. 'Because we are all in a hurry,' he said, pointing to the one other person sitting in the waiting room. I noticed that she was the chairman's private secretary, so I remarked, 'If I were the chairman, you wouldn't have banged on the door like that.' His answer astonished me: 'I most certainly would, wouldn't I?' he retorted, turning to the secretary. 'Yes, I'm afraid he would,' was her reply (the manager missed the irony of the word 'afraid'). The man was simply a bully. Yet two months later, the chairman was gone and the manager in question was promoted to just one rung below the board of directors. A new era had begun; the old culture was giving way to something new, something ruthless, but not more effective in the long term.

Luckily in business you do not meet such individuals very often. If you do, try to confront them head on, like I did. They are not used to this and will be taken aback. If they have been rude, speak to them alone, face to face. If that is not possible, send them an e-mail, politely insisting on respect and courtesy, especially towards your staff. Point out to them that perhaps they were tired or upset, but 'in future please try to contain your emotions, as they may cause offence'. Don't be afraid to act: in normal circumstances, you will never be dismissed or demoted for being polite and frank. Admittedly, there is always a slight risk, but I have confronted people on several occasions and have never been reprimanded for it. If you fail to set a standard of respect for yourself, how can you set one for your team?

There is nothing wrong with being a 'nice guy' in business. The world is full of nice managers and professionals. But there is a big difference between being nice and being weak.

Weak Managers

A weak manager is the worst manager you can possibly have. They are inconsistent, ineffective, not respected and the target of ridicule and blame. As a result, the faults of others are often attributed to the weak manager. If you suspect yourself of being weak (e.g., doing things that you do not agree with, just to please the person who asks), you should either seek professional retraining or change your job.

Most managers make the same mistakes early on in their careers, when they try to become the perfect boss. They want to please everyone and they want to be liked. However, the wise ones quickly learn that if you want to successfully manage a large team of people, you can only (at best) expect to be respected - and even then only for part of the time. Being liked is not a qualification that any self-respecting manager should aim for.

Tough Managers

People generally prefer to work for people they respect, but not necessarily like. Most employees would not choose their bosses as friends or sexual partners (although this does, of course, happen from time to time). If a manager gets too friendly with a subordinate, all kinds of jealousies and internal disputes can arise, until the situation becomes unsustainable.

It may seem ironic, but it is mostly strong managers who are liked, even though they are focused primarily on their goals and the necessary means to achieve them – even if this requires the restructuring or relocation of the team.

Inflexible Managers

The world and its markets are changing faster than ever. In these circumstances, it will be the inflexible managers who find it hardest to keep up and who will need to be replaced. There are two main reasons for inflexibility: weakness (the fear of imposing one's will or strategy on others) and stubbornness (the inability to listen, learn and adapt).

I have formulated what I consider to be the seven characteristics of a really bad manager. It is not a scientific exercise, but it certainly matches my experience:
1. inconsistency ;
2. inflexibility ;
3. bad communicator ;
4. lazy ;
5. lack of resourcefulness and/or imagination ;
6. low intelligence ;
7. hypocritical.

A good manager is:
1. a good decision-maker ;
2. considerate, a person who genuinely tries to do their best for their staff by placing them in the right positions, according to their abilities ;
3. consistent, someone who knows what they want and looks to others to deliver it ;
4. always respectful and polite ;
5. well structured and organized ;
6. someone who appreciates high quality work and can inspire commitment ;
7. tough and never weak.

PEOPLE WHO DO NOT WANT SOLUTIONS

It is important to remember that there are many people who simply do not want solutions. They live in a world where problems give them something to moan about, something to argue and curse over with their neighbours and friends, something to make them feel important or needed. These people are rarely the friends of interim managers or entrepreneurs! By definition, if an entrepreneur is the accelerator, then these people are the brakes.

> **Tip**
> *Whatever you do, when you have a recurrent problem, stay well away from those people who prefer to find problems in solutions instead of solutions to problems.*

During my career, I have met many people who have walked into very positive meetings and completely wrecked them by introducing a hitherto unknown and largely imaginary problem. They invent a theory, which they then develop into an issue, with complex reasons why the solution on the table will never work. They do this to show everyone present how clever they are and to re-establish their authority within the group. These are insecure people, who long to be recognised and to be taken seriously.

There is a huge difference between intelligent questioning (including the playing of devil's advocate, presenting the other side of an issue in order to consider all viewpoints and to eliminate any risks which may have been overlooked) and deliberately creating confusion and complexity. It is all a question of motive. Is the difficult, obstructive or negative person genuinely looking for a better solution or are they just seeking attention and praise? If you suspect them of being deliberately obstructive, stop the meeting immediately, take them outside and ask them bluntly if they are more interested in assisting or hindering the search for a solution. They need to decide - and to decide quickly.

4. Pragmatic Management Tools and Guidelines

BUILDING AND NURTURING A SOCIAL NETWORK

Many professional people assume that building a social network is about meeting potential clients and developing sales leads. This is a misconception. Right from the very beginning, we should build our networks on a basis of knowledge, access to information and opportunities. This means that at a networking event we should not only be looking for new clients or investors but also for people with skill sets that we can utilize – not necessarily as potential employees, but as advisors, consultants or simply friends. However, we can only do this effectively if we know what we are looking for.

Imagine, for example, that you need specialist advice on exporting electronic goods to Asia. If you have a quiet word with the organizer of a networking event, you will be amazed at how quickly you are introduced to the right person – or if not to the right person, then at least to someone who knows someone who can help you .

THE STORY OF THE MARKETING DIRECTOR

I was once invited to a football match by the manager of the investment wing of a large European bank. I was having a splendid supper in the directors' box and sitting beside me was the marketing director of a successful high technology company. He asked me what I knew about doing business in South Korea. I told him about my experience and that the company I was working for had just taken a majority stake in a Korean holding (this was in the late 1990s, when the Korean economy was falling apart). When he asked why, I told him that the company we had purchased was complementary to ours, was well established, making a profit and very well positioned for moving further into Asia. I told him that companies could be acquired for almost next to nothing and that as long as you did not want to take your cash out in a hurry, then you had nothing to lose. 'Korea is not going to float away or disappear,' I said. ' The economy will recover and, when it does, you will be in a very strong position.'

Six months later I heard that my dinner companion's company had made a major acquisition in South Korea and that the transaction had proved extremely successful. Of course, it was no coincidence that we were sitting next to each other that night at the football. The bank's head of corporate investment for the high-technology sector knew that to get my companion to join them for dinner he had to have an attraction. The attraction was not the football or the fine meal - it was me! Or at least the knowledge that I could pass on for free!.

Useful tips on networking events:

1. Be selective. If you are building a career or are in a growth business, you need to allocate at least two evenings a week for corporate entertainment, business meetings and networking events. However, you need to make sure that the participants of a network event are likely to include people who are on your 'required' list. Clubs and societies (such as the Rotary) can be very useful and fulfilling on a personal level, but they tend to be rather closed and inward looking. Moreover, investing too much time in one small local group is not necessarily going to add the same amount of value in the long term as selecting a wider range of events.

2. Eat before you go! Do not miss out on valuable contact opportunities simply because you have not eaten all day. People hogging the food tend to stand out in the crowd. In addition, talking whilst eating is not generally a good idea.

3. Drinking is fine in moderation, but if you arrive on an empty stomach, you will soon feel the champagne's effect on your powers of thought and communication. This may be acceptable at a party, but it can be fatal in a situation where using your wits and emotional intelligence are the key to success.

4. Remember to take your business cards and a smart pen. Do not pull out a cheap biro or a half-chewed pencil to write with. Read any visitor card you receive attentively. If you write something down, do it in a smart pocket notebook, in your PDA or on the back of the card – but never on the front of the card (people have probably spent a fortune on its design and layout, so it is rude to scribble all over it).

5. Do not place newly received business card in a case with other people's cards (you'll look like a card collector). Put it away discreetly and respectfully in your pocket.

6. Make a written or mental list of your needs in terms of advice (legal, business, strategic, HR, finance, etc.) and/or opportunity (supplier, client, distributor, financier).

7. Charm the organizer and let them know your requirements. For example: 'I am thinking about entering the Japanese market and I would like to meet someone with experience in exporting to Japan.'

8. Arrive early and ask to look at the invitation list when you go in. Identify the people who could be of interest to you. If you do not know them, ask one of the receptionists to let the persons concerned know that you are interested in meeting them. Give the receptionist your card and write the name of the person you want to meet on the back, so that when the person arrives the receptionist can point you out.

9. Do not be too pushy. Remember that your aim is to talk a little and listen a lot. Be polite and attentive. Do not monopolise their attention (they want to circulate as well). Keep things brief, but arrange a meeting to explore your ideas further, if they are interested.

10. Remember that the person who you are talking to might only be one step away from the person who you really need to meet, so that even if they cannot be of direct help, they may be able to introduce you to someone who can.

11. At the end of the evening, make a point of saying goodbye to the organizer and thanking them for the invitation. Try to ensure that you will be welcome to return in future. Even if it was a poor event, the decision to come back should be yours – and not the organizer's.

12. Remember that the organizer has a thick address book: make sure you are in it and have access to it.

13. If you do not know anyone, do not stand in the background all evening, but attach yourself to a group of people. If necessary, start a conversation with a complete stranger. Read their lapel badge first and ask an open question, which requires a full answer. An example of such a question might be: 'I notice you work for IBM;, how is the slow down in the Asian economy affecting business?'

14. Always try and steer the conversation in a direction that genuinely interests you. If your conversation partner does not know anything about your question, at least you might be able to ask them who in their organization might be able to help. However, you should only do this after you have asked them a more relevant question and taken an interest in what they have to say.

15. Try and avoid the 'stars' of the evening. They are hard to reach and it is not really worth the time and effort, unless you have something very relevant for them.

16. Sometimes you can write your query in advance. For example, on the front of your card you could write PTO (please turn over) and on the back you could add keywords like 'interested in exporting to Japan'.

COPING WITH CULTURAL DIFFERENCES

Interim managers have to work for companies with very different cultures and, consequently, they need to adapt their approach accordingly. However, sometimes they may find themselves working on assignments where two contrasting cultures meet (especially in merger and acquisition projects). Coping with the differences in these circumstances can be very demanding.

A classic case of culture difference, which I was experienced at first hand, involved the takeover of a division of a large global specialty products company by a medium-sized global petrochemical and polyurethane business.

THE STORY OF BETA AND EXCELSIOR

Excelsior Products (name changed), the takeover target, used to be a successful and profitable company, but over the years its position had weakened and at the time of the proposed takeover was on the point of bankruptcy. Beta International (name changed), the acquiring company, was famous for inventing polystyrene boxes. I was working for Beta, heading up a massive change management project that was the brainchild of the Global IT Director. My project team was going around the world, replacing everyone's personal computer (i.e., removing their freedom) and substituting them with 'thin client' terminals, connected to centrally managed IT systems.

The only hardware that the employees had left on their desks was a screen, a keyboard and a mouse. They could no longer choose what software they wanted to install and they couldn't even display photos of their family and friends as screensavers on their monitors. The project was also reclaiming more than half of all laptops issued to staff, because the new technology allowed employees to log on to their office systems from any computer anywhere in the world, so long as it had an internet connection. The project even took away their personal printers and replaced them with centrally

---

located, multifunctional machines. On one site there were 184 printers for a total of 180 people! The change meant that the employees now had to get up off their backsides and walk across to the printer, instead of just leaning across their desks. A small inconvenience, you might think, but from a change management perspective the removal of the printers proved to be the most challenging aspect of the whole project.

You might assume that the employees of Beta International hated their new 'thin client' technology, but you would be wrong. Of course, in the beginning everyone was afraid and there was strong resistance (but this mainly originated from within the IT department itself, because the changes meant the potential loss of many local IT support engineers and managers). The majority of users were unreservedly grateful, because their old systems were slow and had limited functionality. The new system gave them access to far more information and allowed them to share data with colleagues overseas much faster and more easily. Nevertheless, the political infighting within the IT department continued and was exacerbated by a recent change in the company's structure. Moreover, the arrival of the new acquisition on the scene was destined to have a very unexpected effect on the global roll-out project.

So how does all this relate to the acquisition? Excelsior Products was a world leader in its specialist products. Their culture was one of 'We are the best, we are different' (and indeed many of their employees genuinely believed that they had been purchased because they were the best). However, in reality the company was broke – they had great products and revenue streams, but hopelessly spiralling costs over several years had brought the business to its knees. Beta International was planning to turn this around - and fast.

Excelsior Products spent five times more per employee on its ICT budget than Beta International. By incorporating the new radical thin-client technology, Beta International had the potential to cut Excelsior's ICT costs dramatically. Moreover, Excelsior had changed hands several times in recent years. As a result everyone's job was in doubt, so that convincing them to change was not likely to be as challenging as it had been for Beta International.

However, a unique situation occurred. In Australia two offices, one from Excelsior and one from Beta International, were merged into one. Now both groups of employ-

ees were sitting side by side, forming 'one business, one team'. Interestingly, the Beta International employees were generally happy with the new thin client technology but the Excelsior employees were very disappointed. As a result they complained loudly, much to the bemusement of their Beta colleagues.

What was the problem? In the past, Beta were used to very slow and unreliable systems and they genuinely appreciated the fact that they now had access to information directly from their other offices around the world. However, the Excelsior employees had always had the fastest, most reliable and most high-performance tools, even though they had not been able to share data, due to the incompatibility of their software applications. For Excelsior, cost was never considered an issue. For Beta, cost had become everything.

Excelsior was poor to the point of going under, while Beta was booming and in acquisition mode. The question lay before us – what should we do? Adjust to meet Excelsior expectations or drive on with Beta's improved systems? The whole debate was hampered by unreliable technical support information which clouded the entire issue. In the end, clear communication and strong expectation management calmed the situation. Small compromises were made and the Excelsior employees learned to adapt. For the rest of the deployment project, all the teams were better prepared and a potential disaster was avoided.

Beta International was a company whose culture was based on the principles of the underdog inventor, who made his own way through life, spending his money wisely and honestly. Excelsior was a company that always believed itself to be the Rolls-Royce of adhesives – they found reasons to justify a budget and they spent it. For this reason, it is probably fair to say that the respective cultures of the two companies played a major role in their respective success and failure. Even the biggest empires come crashing down, if they allow themselves to be deluded by their own greatness.

Today, Excelsior is part of a fully integrated Beta International company and is doing very well. Their products are more aligned and their expenditure in line with their earnings. Their in-house talk is now more about how to match client needs and increase profitability, rather than which department can have the biggest budget.

The four bad things about entrepreneurs

There are four very common negative traits in entrepreneurs:

1. They get bored very easily.
2. They are often 'lazy' or quick to lose interest. They are happy to dream up fantastic schemes and ideas, but as soon as their schemes need working through, they no longer want to be bothered about 'the details'.
3. They possess excessive self-belief (some might call it arrogance), which inhibits them from listening and learning, and prevents them from taking good advice when they most need it.
4. They are excessively optimistic, which means that they prefer to believe in the 'golden' new deal which will solve all their problems (which were somebody else's fault anyway), rather than facing the reality that perhaps they were wrong and that prudence might sometimes be a better policy.

Entrepreneurs generally work hard but seldom on the right things at the right time. If they are working on a business plan, it is often too late. In fact, the plan was more than likely the work of someone else and they have just stepped in at the last minute, to challenge the occasional premise or boost the figures.

If you have a CEO who matches this description, the sooner you can ease him out of daily operations the better. Place him in an executive think tank, where he can be encouraged to develop ideas and where he has access to analysts, who can build business cases around them.

How to tell the difference between real and fake entrepreneurs.

(A light-hearted, fictional story to illustrate the difference between a real and a fake entrepreneur.)

THE STORY OF THE REAL AND THE FAKE ENTREPRENEURS

One way to tell the difference between a real entrepreneur and a fake one is to lure them into a dark café alone, supply them with enough alcohol to get them comfortably drunk and then pop the question: 'What is your all time favourite album?' Nine

---

times out of ten, the real entrepreneur (assuming he is aged between 45 and 60) will say 'Pink Floyd, Dark Side of the Moon' and begin singing 'Money, it's a hit. Don't give me that do goody good bullshit!'

Ask the same question to a fake entrepreneur and he will look at you with a slightly annoyed expression, because you have interrupted his flow. He will think for a while and then mutter glibly 'Soft Machine 3', before immediately continuing to bore you with just how grateful the world will be when he finally gets his brilliant product onto the market and just how stupid the established multi-nationals in his field really are.

The real entrepreneur will later ask you to call a taxi for him and will leave you to pay the bill, while the fake will insist on paying for the drinks and invite you to dinner, because he genuinely believes that you just might be the person who understands exactly where he is coming from!

A fake entrepreneur has all the characteristics of a real entrepreneur but is missing two important attributes; namely:

1. In spite of surface appearances, deep down they are not driven by the desire to make money.
2. They lack genuine brilliance and creativity.

Fake entrepreneurs are people who believe that they are successful, even when they clearly are not. They believe that they are right and that everyone else is wrong (or inferior). They are lazy when it comes to analyzing real data and carrying out the necessary monitoring of their company with due diligence. They easily become bored and get irritated with anyone who does not share their view.

A person who struck it lucky with one bright idea, from which he made a pile of cash, is not necessarily a 'real' entrepreneur. A real entrepreneur is able to repeat his success, not necessarily every time but at least with a better than average chance.

A real entrepreneur needs the following attributes:

1. a genuine desire to make money ;
2. intuitive insights and flashes of brilliance ;
3. self-belief ;
4. determination ;

5. charisma (the ability to get others to share their vision) ;
6. willingness to listen and learn ;
7. the ability to make decisions and to take risks.

A real entrepreneur is similar to a fake one, except that they are ready to listen to the opinions of others and usually have an inner circle of objective advisors around them. They are prepared to do almost anything that will produce the required result. They like to know that reality, as they perceive it, is matched by their actual cash flow and their bank balance. If necessary, they will stay up all night, checking budgetary figures line by line, reviewing performance results and overseeing essential monitoring tasks. All entrepreneurs make mistakes, but the successful ones learn from them and do not try to blame them on others.

Whereas psychologists have demonstrated that a 'normal' human being is only prepared to break the law or cheat if they are certain they will not be caught, many entrepreneurs will ignore a law if they think there is a better than even chance of getting away with it.

Entrepreneurs will make up new rules, if the old ones do not suit them. If they do this, they are genuinely surprised when they are challenged by people who stick to the old way of doing things and they simply do not understand what they are supposed to have done wrong! This behaviour is normal to them; in fact, it is probably built into their genes. I don't suppose that there is anything they can do about it (nor would they want to, if there was). They were simply born this way and society has brought their 'strengths' to the surface, by encouraging them to be successful. And a good thing, too. The world needs entrepreneurs: without them mankind would have become extinct long ago.

HANDLING BOREDOM

Many goal-oriented people, especially those with an active imagination, are easily bored. This characteristic can be damaging to even the healthiest entrepreneur, CEO or manager – and to their business.

THE STORY OF THE BORED VET

I once knew a man who had five successful veterinary practices. In total, he had 17 vets working all hours of the day and night, generating substantial revenues. Unfortunately, after a number of years of growth, he became bored. His targets –and his expectations - had been met and his youthful passion for quality of service had given way to a growing lack of personal interest. He also became rather overweight and during a short-lived health drive to lose weight, he was offered the chance to buy an ageing sports club.

Nothing in his background had prepared him for completing a detailed business analysis. His personal boredom had driven him to seek a new challenge, so when he found an opportunity that not only seemed to promise new revenues, glamour and even an improvement in his personal health, he did not carry out the usual scrutiny that he would normally have applied to his core business.

The result was predictable. Buying in at the end of the 1990s, he borrowed money from the bank to finance the acquisition. Unfortunately, his assets were mostly in housing, which coincidentally was declining in value rapidly, due to a change in government policy on tax relief for property financing. The financial boom was over, people were being more careful with their money and they were no longer automatically renewing memberships for clubs they seldom visited. As a result, he found himself the proud owner of a sports club with a swiftly declining membership and high overheads. The net financial and emotional impact was nearly enough to threaten the very core of his veterinary practices. The hoped-for revenues from new membership in the club never materialised and the maintenance and management costs - not to mention the disappearing stocks of alcohol and cash from the till when he wasn't around,- nearly destroyed his core business.

The moral of the cautionary tale is that an entrepreneur should never risk his core business. When they get bored and want to try something new, let them take up fishing.

If you are expecting the entrepreneurs in your organisation to carry out the necessary measures to solve your current problems, you are likely to be sorely disappointed. True entrepreneurs are only interested in final solutions and the benefits they will bring. Working through the fine detail of problem management may amuse them for an hour or two, but no more. After this they will quietly hand over the job to the project managers and the logistics teams. It is much more likely that one day they will come bounding into the office with a great new idea. It might be an idea inspired by boredom or it might be the idea that will make them fantastically rich. Or it might be the idea that finally destroys the business that the company 'doers' have been working so hard to make consistently profitable. One thing is certain: whatever the idea, it will not be the visionary entrepreneur who hangs around to personally ensure that all the details are covered: that is work for the operations team!

THE STORY OF THE FLYING CEO

I was once the COO of a high-tech software company and its strategy was most at risk when the CEO returned to the office after a long intercontinental flight. The ideas that he dreamed up after several hours of sleep deprivation in the economy section of a Boeing 747 were sometimes seriously alarming. If it was not for his team of trustworthy advisors, he would have gone bankrupt a dozen times or more.

WORKING HOURS AND EFFICIENCY

Because of the ever increasing tendency towards globalization, many projects now need to be coordinated with teams in different time zones. For this reason – but also to cater for modern domestic life patterns - I am in favour of 'liberalising' working hour structures to meet the needs of individuals. However, I still insist on 'core hours' in each time zone, which means I require office attendance between 1000 and 1500 hours local time (whenever possible). Outside these hours, the use of modern, web-based remote access technology allows people to work from any location they please – and at any time. I have nothing against people working remotely, sometimes for days at a time. However, it needs to be managed properly and only works well with socially responsible people, who have the discipline to focus on their work.

The biggest problem is how to avoid setting trends which may eventually weaken the core feeling of the 'team concept' and make communication more difficult. For companies whose cultures are not used to home working, there is the tendency not to contact someone when they are out of the office. It is almost as if home workers somehow seem to disappear off the face of the earth. This can be handy if they need some quiet time to write up their reports, etc., but it can also reduce efficiency dramatically, if their colleagues forget that they are working as normal, but only from another location. This can even apply when working from a different office within the same building.

In general, the benefits of home working technologies outweigh the disadvantages. For example, it does seem a criminal waste of resources that employees are required to take half a day's leave to wait at home for a service company to fix or deliver something, when web-based office working can remove this obstacle. If you are paranoid about whether your remote workers are really working, there are plenty of sophisticated monitoring tools to judge their performance, if your internal reporting structures are too weak to detect time-wasters.

In my experience, when people are given the ability to work on their office systems from home (or from any other location), productivity increases dramatically. You would be surprised how many people log on to work after the children have been put to bed or when there is simply nothing good on the television. I know many people who spend their last day of their holidays reading e-mails and booking meetings, in preparation for returning to work.

If you want to retain your staff, it is important that their families should also come to see that their breadwinner's employer is not a monster, ever-demanding yet never satisfied. Part-time home working can help to improve this perception. Moreover, too many of us are commuting to work on congested highways, only to arrive at our destination at the same time as everyone else. For many organisations, this method of working is already unnecessary and outdated.

Citrix systems have given us the ability to work 'anywhere, anytime, any place'. Linked into the standard Microsoft platforms, their technology utilizes the power of the internet and of wireless communication, with extremely effective results.

It seems pointless that we should put our health and our family lives at risk by working excessive hours away from home, when it is no longer really necessary. We are forcing ourselves to leave for work earlier and earlier each morning, in a desperate attempt to beat the rush hour, only returning home after another gruelling drive at the end of the day. (In fact, the term 'rush hour' has become outdated and now needs to be changed in many countries across the globe, since the 'hour' now covers about four hours in the morning and the same period in the evening.) The waste of fuel and the damage to the environment is staggering – and unjustifiable. Sadly, however, man is slow to change and the new technologies, such as Citrix, are still likely to take many years before they become standard.

A FINAL TIP TO SOLVING PROBLEMS

Sometimes the most obvious solutions to your problems are staring you in the face, but you simply cannot see them. Normally, I like to think of myself as someone who notices things and people often say that I seem to have a comment or observation for almost everything I see and hear. I am still not certain, whether this is a compliment or a criticism!

Yet even I am not always as observant as I should be. It was only recently that I discovered that the piece of plastic on the top of the washing-up mop is actually there for a reason! I always find this flap annoying, when trying to clean the inside of wine glasses, but just the other day I found my wife scraping the bottom of a baking tray with it, removing encrusted grime most effectively, without damaging the protective non stick layer!

Why is it that people cannot see the obvious solution to a problem that is right in front of them? The answer is that the closer you are to something, the less you are able to see of it. The further away you are, the clearer it becomes. From a distance, you can differentiate things. Consequently, the secret to effective observation is to select how far you wish to be from any given issue or problem. Moreover, you also have the additional option of zooming in or zooming out, as the situation demands (although many people zoom in too quickly and, once in, forget to zoom back out again).

The difference between 'Don't get involved' and 'Why didn't you do something?' is small, yet its impact on a business can be enormous. For managers - and especially interim managers, who do not always know the people around them that well - the judgement between helping and interfering is often a difficult one. The secret is to remain objective, closely observing the body language and other signs given by those more closely involved. You need to step back and watch, rather than step in and take over. You need to resist the urge to show people how clever and how experienced you are. After all, you cannot do everything alone, nor can you be everywhere all the time. Letting those around you find their own way is often a painful yet necessary reality.

An old woman beating the living daylights out of her assailant with her handbag and umbrella may not need (or welcome) your assistance. On the other hand, remaining passive when a situation is clearly crying out for help is simply not acceptable - especially when you know that your intervention can make a difference. Age and experience teach us to make these judgements more accurately as the years go by, but the bottom line is that you must not be led by your ego but by your ability to judge quickly what assistance you can offer. Will it make a difference and will it be welcome?

In life, there are no fixed rules. Whatever I say in this book, someone somewhere else will be saying precisely the opposite. All I ask is that you read my theories and observations with an open mind, think about them and then decide for yourself whether my way is the way for you. Whatever conclusions you reach, I wish you lots of fun and lots of success in tackling the challenges posed by your clients' problems. And remember: when you walk away from a company at the end of an assignment, you should only consider the job well done if the client's problem has already left before you.

Good luck,
Harley

P.S. Don't forget to visit the www.making-a-difference.be website and the Manager's Forum blog. The publishing team and I are very interested in your comments and feedback, especially any stories about how this book might have helped you in one way or another. Your suggestions are always welcome!

Glossary

Balanced score card A performance monitoring system displayed on a single card. Originally the BSC was designed to ensure that a business could measure its performance in all areas (Sales, Marketing, Finance, Production, HR, etc.). It enabled the management team to monitor very simply the entire performance of the business against predefined targets and thus ensure it was in balance and moving in the right direction. A brilliant concept but unfortunately rather complex to implement. I use a very simplified version to identify the performance of a small number of important aspects of a project and to ensure alarm signals are raised early on.

Buy-in The amount of support one achieves. If you have 'buy-in', this means that people agree with your plan and support you in your project.

CAPEX Capital Expenditure is the allocation of funds for the purchase of 'capital' items, such as new machinery, tools and other items that the company can classify as 'assets' on the balance sheet. Capital expenditure can be written off against tax and depreciates over a period of time (depending on local tax laws). For example, a new computer is a capital expense and it therefore shows in the bookkeeping as having a specific value, which normally decreases to zero over 3-5 years.

Citrix Citrix is a software company that makes software to enable the thin client systems to work. It is a kind of middleware that allows end users to work on almost any kind of computing device, anywhere around the globe, exactly as if they were sitting behind their own PC in the office. Citrix has now developed a whole range of very useful products for modern offices and for people on the move. See www.citrix.com

Dominant coalition The dominant coalition is the group of people that make the real decisions within a company and effectively run it. Sometimes the members of the coalition are not named on the official organization chart. However, in normal circumstances they usually comprise part of the senior management 'leadership' team or the board of directors, or a combination of both. I once knew a secretary who worked herself into positions of unbelievable decision-making power, planting ideas into her boss's head and confirming them in e-mails as his decisions. She ran the company agenda, scrutinized every meeting plan and became so formidable that no one dared to challenge her. The good news for the business was that although she never admitted to having authority, she was, in fact, doing an extremely good job as the 'shadow' CEO. I would certainly consider her as part of the dominant coalition.

Firmware The software that runs a device, such as a mobile phone or PDA (personal digital assistant).

Follow the sun This is an expression used by multi-national companies when they want to have a service that literally follows the sun. I.e. when a service stops at the end of a working day in one geographical location, it is taken over by another unit located in the following time zone, thus creating a 24 hour a day service around the world.

Gantt chart A Gantt chart is a project plan (commonly used by Microsoft in their application MS Project), showing resources, tasks, timelines, milestones, deliverables, etc.

Gardening leave Time off given to employees when there services are no longer required but they still remain on the payroll.

| KPI | Key Performance Indicator. A quantifiable method to determine a specific performance result. For example, if your project has to deliver a minimum amount of savings equivalent to 1M€ per year, the KPI might be set as a range from 1M€ - 3 M€ per year. |

| Milestones | A milestone is a significant marker point in a project. It is always linked to a specific point in time and/or to a specific level of expenditure. A milestone is required to set targets and to assess progress in comparison with the planning. |

| NPV | Net Present Value. In layman's terms, this is the value that your investment or project will realize, taking into account all costs and revenue. Many companies compare this figure with what the same outlay in cash would yield if invested in recognized 'traditional' investments. Any investment or project that does not at least match the standard return on investment needs to have an extremely good reason for going ahead. |

| OPEX | Operational Expenditure. This is the expenditure that a company incurs in its normal day-to-day operations. It is sometimes referred to as 'overheads'. Operational expenditure is more or less predictable and is budgeted on the basis of actual costs from a previous year. (It is in the interests of most companies to keep OPEX as low as possible, as it directly impacts on profit). |

| PMI | PMI is an abbreviation of the name of the Project Management Institute. PMI is widely known for its project methodology structure, which is in general use throughout Europe and the US. There are courses held, offering certification in PMI. This certification is a very good starting point for interim managers and would-be project managers. It is sometimes criticized for being a little 'top heavy' in certain circumstances but companies can adapt it to their needs. |

| Prince 2 | Prince 2 is a rival project management methodology to PMI. Perhaps a little more pragmatic but less all inclusive. |

Project gates   Gates are the point in a project which mark a significant change in activity or where approval is required before proceeding to the next stage. For example, when the design stage is finished, you may decide to have a gate to give approval to move on to the fabrication or development stage.

Project Steering Committee   An appointed group which oversees or 'steers' the project in the right direction, ensuring that scope creep is avoided. The Steering Committee or Project Board is usually responsible for all major decisions and for monitoring the budgets and deliverables. It is often made up of members who are also 'sponsors' i.e. the investors who have provided the project budget.

SME   Small to medium-sized enterprise.

Solution architecture phase   Solution architecture is the phase of a project (sometimes called the detailed design phase) where the solution is designed and put down on paper. It can also be referred to the 'blue print', showing how all the systems work together, etc.

Thin client   A thin client is a piece of IT technology. In fact, it is a kind of terminal which links the end user's screen, mouse and keyboard to a remote central computer system, where their applications run and where their data is stored. Thin clients are very cheap and extremely reliable, as they need very little computing power. Consequently, their shelf life is much longer than that of a standard PC, they use far less energy and they do not need regular updating or any local onsite maintenance.

WBS   WBS (work book structure) is another term for an aspect of a Gantt chart. It is basically the terminology used for each phase of the project and their timings etc.